JAMES MONROE
Public Claimant

JAMES MONROE
Public Claimant

LUCIUS WILMERDING, Jr.

RUTGERS UNIVERSITY PRESS
New Brunswick   New Jersey

To Jane

Preface

In this small book I shall examine two questions that greatly concerned Monroe during the years that lay between his retirement from the Presidency in 1825 and his death in 1831. The first relates to his pecuniary claims against the United States; the second, to his character for integrity in the management of public money.

Neither of these questions has hitherto engaged the attention of his biographers. Although they have mentioned his claims in a general way and deplored the failure of Congress to allow them in full, they have not bothered to particularize them, nor have they furnished their readers with any standards whereby to judge them; indeed, it is all too obvious that they have not understood them. As to the transactions and proceedings that led Monroe in 1825 to defend himself from accusations of embezzlement, his faithful biographers, or eulogists, have said not a word. Monroe might not have approved their vagueness or their silence. Upon leaving the Presidency, he invited investigation; and he announced with an admirable, if deceptive, show of candor: "In what relates to both objects, I ask no favor, nor do I appeal to generous motives. I ask nothing but justice."

In writing of these obscure topics, indissolubly joined by Monroe himself, I have had a double purpose. I have meant to illustrate a side of Monroe's character that has hitherto lain in the shadows; but I have meant also to throw light upon the early mode of paying public ministers for their services abroad, the rules of office governing the settlement of their accounts at the Treasury, and the remedies open to them when they were dissatisfied with the settlements. It has been my observation that very few historians or biographers have any clear ideas on these matters; unfamiliar with the law and usage, they make all sorts of mistakes in explaining the accounts of individuals with the public. I would hope to help them avoid such mistakes in the future; but I am painfully aware that the routine of official business is not an inspiring subject of study. It is, perhaps, only in the telling of such bizarre stories as that of James Monroe and his claims that even a professional writer, let alone the general reader, can be made to swallow such unpalatable information.

One chapter of this book, in a slightly different form, has appeared in the *New-York Historical Society Quarterly* for April 1960. The rest is new.

Lucius Wilmerding, Jr.

Princeton, N. J.
May, 1960

Contents

JAMES MONROE
Public Claimant

1

An Extraordinary Request

On the sixth of January 1825 the members of the House
of Representatives were greatly surprised to receive from
the President of the United States a message, addressed
to themselves and the Senate jointly, asking or demanding
that all matters of account and claims between himself and
his country, spread over a period of more than forty years,
be now examined by Congress with a view to an eventual
settlement. "I have been," wrote Mr. Monroe, "long in the
service of my country, and in its most difficult conjunc-
tures, as well abroad as at home, in the course of which I
have had a control over the public moneys to a vast amount.
If, in the course of my service, it shall appear, on the most
severe scrutiny, which I invite, that the public have sustained any loss by any act of mine, or of others, for which
I ought to be held responsible, I am willing to bear it. If,
on the other hand, it shall appear, on a view of the law,
and of precedents, in other cases, that justice has been with-

held from me, in any instance, as I have believed it to be in many, and greatly to my injury, it is submitted whether it ought not to be rendered." [1]

Such was the burden of the message; but what did it mean? Few members took seriously Monroe's own explanation that he wanted to establish a precedent for the future protection of the public and of such individuals as might rise to the executive magistracy. He had suggested, indeed, that no one in his situation could expect to enjoy undisturbed tranquillity and peace in his retirement unless his conduct in all pecuniary concerns were placed by severe scrutiny on a basis not to be shaken; and he had intimated that, in the future movements of the government, the knowledge that such scrutiny would be made must form a new and strong barrier against the abuse of the public confidence. But these explications were more specious than revealing; nor were they well calculated to gull a body of men long practiced in befogging particular designs with a cloud of generalities.

Some members conjectured that the President wished to free himself from certain aspersions that had been cast upon his character. They recollected that at the last two sessions of Congress some hints had been dropped that at least a portion of his pecuniary transactions with an agent of the public required explanation. But they remembered also that when he had been asked to appear before the committee of the House that was investigating the defalcations of this agent, he had desired the person who brought him the message to tell the chairman of the committee, General

John Cocke of Tennessee, that he was a scoundrel and that that was the only answer he would give him.[2]

Other members detected a claim for money. As to the nature of the claim, they expressed, indeed, the most conflicting opinions. All might agree that it was a demand founded in equity; for had it been a simple matter of account, the President would have gone to the accounting officers of the Treasury. But the President's friends surmised that he was merely asking for the removal of such legal obstacles as might stand in the way of the just settlement of an unliquidated pecuniary claim; his enemies thought, and dared say, that he was seeking to use the influence of high official station in order to command the attention of Congress and obtain a favorable settlement of doubtful accounts. A few members, more cautious or more ignorant, professed or pretended a total want of ability to discover his object.[3]

In point of fact, Monroe had a double object. Stung by the obliquitous remarks of his detractors in the matter of the mysterious disappearance of $20,000 of public money from the accounts of Colonel Samuel Lane, Commissioner of Public Buildings, who in many affairs, public and private, had acted as his agent, he wished to put his conduct in a proper light. And conceiving himself to have been badly treated in the settlement of the accounts of his two missions to Europe—that commencing in 1794 under Washington and that of 1803 under Jefferson—he wished to present a long and complex claim to Congress.[4] But these two motives, as the event was to show, operated upon his mind with very unequal degrees of force. In defense of his honor he would be content to lay his explanations before the committee raised to receive them; he would never insist that Congress express an opinion on them or even hear the testimony on the other side. In defense of his pocket, however, he would never rest until he had extracted from the Treasury the very last dollar that he considered due him— or until death should prevent his further striving.

The preoccupation of the President with his monetary grievances was not unnatural. To repel the insinuations of his adversaries he had only to prove the innocence of his dealings with Colonel Lane and patiently to expect the acquittance of Congress or the oblivion of time. But his need for cash was immediate; for in 1825 Monroe stood at the verge of bankruptcy.

Thirty years of public service had injured him severely in his private fortune. "I was at no time rich," he would inform the public in 1826. "My landed inheritance in Westmoreland County was small, but still it was something. By the sale and investment of the amount received for it in other lands, as soon as I arrived at maturity, I had laid the foundation of independence, and should have attained it had I pursued the profession of the law a few years longer; for I possessed, at the time of my appointment on my first mission to France of 1794, more property than I now hold, and owed comparatively nothing." [5] As he prepared to lay down the office of President, the prospect before him was bleak. Much of his property had been swept away, his hold upon the rest was precarious, and he was deeply in debt not only to the Bank of the United States and to Baring Brothers but also to a multitude of private individuals.

His urgent need for money might also explain the generality and the vagueness of his message to Congress. Every petitioner is anxious that his prayer be heard by a sympathetic tribunal. Had Monroe urged his demands in a precise and distinct form, the House of Representatives would probably have divided the message and referred so much of it as related to his official conduct to a select committee, and so much of it as related to his accounts to the standing Committee of Claims or to the standing Committee on Foreign Affairs. But the Committee of Claims was governed by rules as inflexible, and almost as well known, as those which regulate a court of chancery; and these rules were not well calculated to produce a favorable report on the President's petition; in addition, the members of the committee, indifferently appointed at the beginning of each Congress, were not noted for their generosity to the public creditors. A reference to the Committee on Foreign Affairs was equally to be avoided. A leading member of that committee, John W. Taylor of New York, had already declined the solicitations of the President to take charge of his message in the House; its chairman, John Forsyth of Georgia, had very grossly made known his belief that Monroe was leagued with Ninian Edwards against William H. Crawford as a candidate for the Presidency.[6]

By requesting a general investigation of his pecuniary transactions with the government, by merely suggesting that during the course of that investigation some claim might arise, some balance be found for or against him, and by giving his petition a double aspect and involving it in considerations of the most delicate nature, the President might hope to secure its reference to a select committee—a committee which would be, on one side, a court of honor and, on the other, a financial body. He might count on himself controlling by a parliamentary maneuver the appointment of the chairman of such a committee; and he could reasonably expect that, out of courtesy, its members would be chosen from amongst his friends.

The timing of his message was also dictated by considerations touching its financial side. In December 1824, Congress was debating a bill to compensate General La Fayette, the nation's guest, for the financial sacrifices made by him in the cause of America during the War of the Revolution. A question of tactics arose in the President's family. His daughter, Mrs. George Hay, anxiously insisted that her father present his claim immediately, before Congress should come to its final determination.[7] But Monroe, better versed in the science or art of public psychology, wisely decided to wait. Doubtless, he agreed with John Quincy Adams that if he were now to push himself forward, he would occasion much animadversion unfavorable to himself and even to his claim. It was not until he had set his hand to an act authorizing the payment to La Fayette of the sum of $200,000, and granting him a township of land, that he invited the attention of Congress to his own case.

His measures had been carefully taken, and at first everything proceeded according to plan. No sooner had his message been read in the House of Representatives than Samuel D. Ingham of Pennsylvania, by prearrangement, moved its reference to a select committee. Ingham had consented, though reluctantly, to undertake the President's business in the House; by moving the committee he would, by custom of the House, be put at the head of it. A counter motion to refer the message to the Committee of Claims was decided in the negative by a large majority, as was a motion to lay it on the table.

But now a difficulty arose. Forsyth of Georgia offered an amendment to Ingham's motion, that the committee be instructed to receive from the President any evidences and explanations which he might think proper to present and to report the same to the House. The design and effect of this amendment was to prevent the committee from making any report, favorable or unfavorable, upon the merits of his claim, or even to report any statement of facts. The supporters of the President justly complained that such instructions would confine the duties of the committee to a clerkship and deprive the President of the benefits which he might expect from a sifting investigation of facts; they noticed truly that he was already amply able to communicate to the House, through the Speaker, any papers he wished to lay before it, and that the appointment of a committee shackled by instructions would come to little more. But their cries were unavailing. The Forsyth amendment was adopted by a vote of 90 to 70, and then the Ingham motion was passed. Monroe communicated his disappointment to John Quincy Adams, to whom he spoke of Forsyth "with moderation, but with a sense of injury." [8]

The appointment of the Ingham committee was the only immediate consequence of the President's joint message, for the Senate, expecting the action of the House, had on January 10, the day of its receipt, laid it on the table. Ingham and his colleagues proceeded promptly to their task, not a very difficult one since they had only to receive from Monroe two memoirs that he had had ready for almost a year. On February 21 the committee reported these memoirs to the House, together with some miscellaneous papers referred to it on the motion of General Cocke.[9] After being read, the report was laid on the table.

The public now, for the first time, became aware of the nature of the charges that the President sought to repel and of the claims that he meant to assert. So incoherent, however, and indeed so uncandid, were his memoirs that few persons could really understand the transactions to which they related or form any opinion as to the propriety of his conduct or the validity of his claims. It is therefore necessary to arrest our narrative and to attempt a statement of facts. We may begin with the matter of the Furniture Fund, an incident in Monroe's life which has escaped the diligence, or been suppressed by the delicacy, of his partial biographers.

II

The Furniture Fund
and Colonel Lane

The Furniture Fund was established by Congress on March 3, 1817, the day before Monroe's inauguration, for the purpose of furnishing the President's House, the reconstruction of which was then nearing completion. It consisted of an appropriation of $20,000 to be expended under the direction of the President himself.

Monroe's first action was to appoint two of his friends, William Lee, Second Auditor of the Treasury, an ostentatious man,[1] and Samuel Lane, Commissioner of Public Buildings, a corrupt one, to manage the business for him. Lee was to digest a plan for furnishing the house, to contract for the articles needed, and to receive them when delivered; Lane was to take charge of the fund and control its disbursements. Both must do the work without commission or additional compensation, for no appropriation had been made, or would be made, to defray the expenses of their agency.[2]

Lee immediately proceeded to review the situation. The furniture in the former structure had been destroyed with it in 1814; except for a few pieces, nothing could be got from the Tayloe house, occupied by President Madison; nor could anything, new or secondhand, be bought in America, suitable for a presidential palace. It would be necessary to order things from abroad, but it was impossible that they could be received in season for the reception of the President in the fall.[3]

Apprized of this difficulty, Monroe suggested a simple solution. He had in the house he had occupied as Secretary of State a small service of excellent plate, made for his own use by the best artists in France and England; he had also dining room, drawing room, and bedroom furniture, French china, and kitchen furniture, most of it purchased abroad, which was adapted to the purpose. He had intended to sell these articles upon leaving the Department of State; but he would now offer them to the government at the price at which they might be valued by two citizens of the first respectability, assisted by persons skilled in the manufacture of each article. He would not, however, expect immediate payment. The whole of the Furniture Fund was needed for purchases abroad. He would, therefore, be content to wait until another appropriation should be made. If that event should not occur, he would retake his furniture and bear the loss occasioned by its use.[4]

An offer made by a principal to himself through an agent is usually accepted. On May 15, 1817, Generals John Mason and John P. Van Ness, aided by experts, valued

Monroe's furniture at $9,071.22½. On the same day the transaction was concluded; Lane paid and Monroe acknowledged the receipt of $9,071.22 "in full of the within account." [5] Lane charged $6,000 to the Furniture Fund and the balance, as we must presume, to a private running account with the President.[6]

The alacrity with which Monroe accepted a payment for which he had undertaken to wait might have occasioned some public criticism, had the facts been known to anyone except Monroe himself and a few friendly clerks. Yet Monroe might have offered a satisfactory defense. He was about to leave Washington on a tour of inspection, or a triumphal progress, which would take him through thirteen states; he had expected to finance this tour by the sale of his furniture; but his hopes had been prevented by the necessity of retaining it. In this situation he had accepted the money from Colonel Lane; but he did not regard it as a final payment in discharge of a debt but as an advance, or non-interest-bearing loan, to be repaid later from his private funds or from a subsequent appropriation. In point of fact, when Monroe returned to Washington in the autumn, he repaid to the Furniture Fund the $6,000 which he had taken out of it.

In the meantime the fund itself had proved inadequate to its object. Furniture had been ordered from France, but the bills were greatly in excess of the estimates. Almost everything, it turned out, had had to be made to order. Two clocks, indeed, had been obtained ready made—almost the only ones in France without nudities; but the furniture for the Oval Room had presented a difficulty. It was desirable to obtain such articles as united strength with elegance, simplicity of design with the richness suitable to the decoration of a house occupied by the First Magistrate of a Free Nation. Mahogany had been specified, but mahogany was not to be had; besides, as the President would be informed by his agents at Le Havre, mahogany was not generally admitted in the furniture of a saloon, even in private gentlemen's houses. Gilt wood, a much more expensive material, had accordingly been substituted, and Bellanger, the first ébéniste in Paris, commissioned to make it up. The change of wood had required also a change in the trimmings of the fauteuils, the draperies of the curtains, and so forth; everything must be richer, that everything might be in harmony. Crimson silks had been bought of Cartier fils and the whole made up by Laveissier, a very good tapissier; but crimson was 50 per cent dearer than any other color.[7]

Monroe, notified of these transactions, found himself faced with the prospect, not only of getting nothing from the government for his private furniture, but of having to meet a deficiency in the Furniture Fund of nearly $11,000. He took the appropriate measures, asked for both a deficiency and a supplemental appropriation, and obtained a further grant to the fund of $30,000. His friend, William Lee, was careful to apprize the proper committees of Congress of the President's generosity in consenting to the public use of his private furniture; but he found no occasion to mention that the President had derived a compensatory benefit from the private use of public funds.[8]

The new appropriation was made on April 20, 1818. On April 24, Monroe wrote to Colonel Lane again offering to make his furniture available for public use.[9] But he no longer suggested a sale. He would retain his furniture until new furniture was procured, on condition that Lane advance him the amount of the valuation to be repaid when that event should happen. The free use of the public money would be an inadequate reparation for the loss he would sustain, and had already sustained, by its use. Lane immediately accepted the offer, readvanced to Monroe the sum of $9,071.22, charged the amount to the Furniture Fund, and took the occasion to declare his opinion in writing that the furniture had been greatly undervalued, that it had been much injured during the winter, and that Monroe should have consented to sell it.[10]

Those who are familiar with the self-serving letters written by lawyers on their own behalf or on that of their clients will not hastily conclude from this correspondence that Monroe had abandoned his idea of selling his furniture to the government. Indeed, he himself later explained that by binding himself to retake his furniture unconditionally and to repay the money received for it, he had meant to guard against the contingency of his death by placing the affair entirely under the control of the government, not doubting, in that event, on a view of all the circumstances, that justice would be done to his family.[11]

Monroe spent the money thus received on further tours of inspection;[12] a continued use was found in the White House for his furniture; and by 1821 he felt justified in translating the advance into a payment. In February of that year he authorized the First Auditor of the Treasury to admit the vouchers relating to this transaction in the settlement of Lane's accounts;[13] and in March of the succeeding year, during Lane's final illness, he added to this authority a positive direction.[14] The Auditor, of course, complied, and in the final settlement of the accounts of the Furniture Fund the sum of $9,071.22 was allowed for the amount paid him for his furniture per receipt and account.

Monroe, however, had taken a final precaution. In directing the Auditor to admit his claim, he had undertaken to regard the payment as merely provisional. Upon leaving office he would bring the affair to the attention of Congress and, if it were not approved by the committee or other authority raised to investigate it, he would annul it, retake his furniture, and repay the whole of the money. To protect the public from loss in the event of his death, he pointed out and formally appropriated the funds from which repayment, if required, could be obtained. He had, so he said, an account against the public for balances due him in his foreign missions, of which the principal item was a claim to extra expenses for his special mission to London, ending in 1807. He would agree to apply whatever sum might be allowed him for this claim—and he could hardly expect to receive less than $4,500—to the payment, so far as it would go, of the amount advanced him on account of his furniture; the furniture itself might then be sold to pay the balance.

The observant reader may perceive in all these dealings nothing really censurable. The President may, indeed, have seemed to be making a contract with himself, inasmuch as he had authority to direct the disbursement of the fund from which he was paid; but the precautions that he had taken to protect the public from loss, and himself from blame, were perhaps adequate. Another of his transactions with the Furniture Fund was, however, less carefully guarded. The articles purchased abroad for the President's House were obtained through the agency of Russell and La Farge, merchants at Le Havre. From this same firm Monroe contemporaneously ordered for his private use 1,200 bottles of champagne and burgundy and some other articles. The bill came out blending these two orders together; but, instead of having them separated and referring to the President the charges which originated from his private order, Colonel Lane, by inadvertence or intent, paid the whole and charged the whole upon the Furniture Fund. The error or fraud was presently detected by the accounting officers of the Treasury and the claims for credit disallowed in the settlement of Lane's account. Of this illegal charge Monroe, however, knew nothing at the time it was made. According to the testimony of Lane's clerk, the bill was settled in this manner without his approbation or knowledge.[15]

These two transactions constitute the solid basis of fact upon which would presently be reared an elaborate superstructure of rumor, fancy, and suspicion. They would never have become known to the public, unless by the disclosures of the President himself, but for the inopportune death of Colonel Lane in 1822. A dead man's accounts must be promptly settled. When it was found that Lane had died insolvent with $20,000 of public money unaccounted for, rumors began to circulate obscurely that the President himself had used large sums of public money and thereby occasioned the defalcation. These rumors were fed by the further discovery that Monroe had kept a private, but unvouchered, running account with Lane and that he was indebted in a large amount to the latter's estate.

The circumstances were peculiar. It had been Monroe's habit, during his absences from Washington, to leave the White House in charge of Colonel Lane. From time to time he would place funds in his hands to purchase articles and pay bills, but he never took receipts nor recorded the amounts. As to the application of the funds, he knew nothing at all; for whenever he asked for a settlement of the account, Lane found means to postpone it. But Monroe was not worried; he supposed that he might owe Lane, but thought that there could not be much difference between them either way. When, on his deathbed, Lane offered a settlement, Monroe declined it: he would not distress his friend with the account in his then situation; whether he lived or died, there could be no difficulty about it.[16]

There *was*, however, a difficulty. When, after Lane's death, the representatives of the two parties came to adjust this private account, they found that the credits greatly exceeded the debits. Lane had not confined his expenditures on Monroe's behalf to the funds supplied him; he had advanced the President money without his request or knowledge. For example, he had supplied large sums of money for the use of the White House to Joseph Jeater, the President's thieving steward; but when the latter had converted the money to his own use, Lane had been afraid to tell the President of the advance.[17] Another transaction might seem even more improper. This was the payment by Lane of an accommodation note for $1,500 that Monroe had in the Patriotic Bank. The circumstances were explained as follows: The bank, in Monroe's absence, called for a curtail of $500; Colonel Lane, a director of the bank, remonstrated; the bank insisted, and Lane, with some warmth, directed that the whole note be charged to him. According to Overton Carr, Cashier of the Patriotic Bank: "This was done without the knowledge of Mr. Monroe, as he was not at that time in the city of Washington." [18] As a consequence of such advances, the balance stated in Lane's favor by those appointed to settle the account exceeded $6,500. Yet, so deficient were the vouchers, that no one could be sure that every item had been entered or correctly charged.[19]

The discovery of the shortage of $20,000 in Lane's public accounts led to a legislative inquiry. In December 1822, a committee was appointed by the House of Representatives to investigate the sale of public lots in Washington; for it was in the management of this business that Lane was thought, and rightly thought, to have perpetrated his frauds. The chairman of this committee, General John Cocke of Tennessee, soon shifted his attention from Lane's transactions with the public to Monroe's transactions with Lane. He evinced a particular interest in the disbursements from the Furniture Fund and in the credits and debits entered in Lane's private account with the President. But when Cocke prepared a report very prejudicial to Monroe, the committee refused to accept it.[20]

At the next session of Congress another committee was appointed, and Cocke was again placed at its head. But though its terms of reference were somewhat wider than before, it again declined to inquire or report what disposition had been made of the $38,000 placed in the hands of Colonel Lane for furnishing the White House, alleging that it was a private transaction between the President and Lane; that as the money was to be expended under the direction of the President, he could appoint whomsoever he pleased as his agent; and that the resolution did not authorize the inquiry.[21] Monroe was in complete agreement. When Cocke invited him to attend the committee or to answer questions in writing, the President refused in insulting terms.[22]

Monroe had escaped investigation, but he had not corrected erroneous impressions nor dispelled doubts. His refusal to explain his private affairs, or to answer the interrogations of a congressional committee looking into the embezzlements of his unfaithful agent, although doubtless occasioned by the indignant disdain of conscious rectitude, did nothing to lighten the dark blot that was spreading over his character. On the contrary, his silence made even more plausible the insinuations and the whispers of an industrious, able, and perhaps malignant opposition. The suspicions of the public were further inflamed when, in the summer of 1824, a committee of Congress, investigating the plot of Ninian Edwards against the presidential candidacy of William H. Crawford, cut off the sworn testimony of Senator James Noble of Indiana immediately after he had stated that Edwards had once told him that Monroe was in his power through the means of Colonel Lane. The stopping of the evidence, as John Quincy Adams foresaw, operated worse on the public mind than if everything had come out.[23]

Such was the situation when, in January 1825, Monroe called upon Congress, as the only proper and competent tribunal, to pass upon his integrity in the pecuniary trusts which the nation had committed to him. The memoir that he sent to the Ingham committee in relation to this subject began in general terms. He had been in the service of the government since 1794. He wished every transaction of his life, in which the public might have any interest, to be investigated with the utmost rigor. There was no occurrence that might not be sifted to the bottom by authentic and original documents or by living testimony. All his books and papers were open to the committee's inspection; in questions of doubt, if there should be any, reference might be made to those of the opposite party. But when Monroe descended to particulars, he greatly narrowed the inquiry. The explanations that he gave, and the letters, bills, vouchers, and accounts that he sent in, regarded only his management of the Furniture Fund and the White House establishment.

By means of this memoir, comprising both observations and documents, Monroe might hope to rehabilitate his character and protect it from further aspersion. The memoir was excellently adapted to its object. The documents were so ill-arranged, and sometimes so irrelevant, that a true statement of facts could be extracted from them only with the greatest difficulty.[24] But the facts were there, and they proved not the guilt but the misfortune of Monroe. The observations, on the other hand, by suppressing some facts, emphasizing others, but misstating none, left the impression that Monroe was not merely blameless and unfortunate but also deserving of the highest applause.

The duties of the presidential office, Monroe explained, were multifarious. They extended from the internal and external administration of the country to the mere signature of patents, of commissions for the army and navy, and of Mediterranean passports. The day was not long enough for one man to perform them with equal attention. A neglect of the higher duties must redound to the injury of the public; of the lower duties, perhaps to that of the President—especially if they involved a pecuniary responsibility. In this situation he, Monroe, had appointed an agent, the Commissioner of Public Buildings, to manage the Furniture Fund and the household establishment. But how could the public lose? The duties had been committed to the person best qualified by the nature of his office to execute them; Colonel Lane had received no public compensation for his agency; his errors, if any, were chargeable to the President. In the meantime, the whole mind and the unceasing labors of the Chief Magistrate had been employed on the great interests of the nation.

As to the sale of his own furniture to the United States, concerning which so much hubbub had been raised, Monroe could show that the public had been in every way a gainer. Not only had he sold it cheap but he had applied the proceeds to a public purpose, the inspection of the country's maritime and inland frontiers, a work of incalculable value to the nation but one that formed no part of his official duties. The committee should also remember that it was in their power, or the power of Congress, to annul the whole transaction. If it were not approved by competent authority, he had promised to retake his furniture and repay the money.

The Ingham committee, confined by its instructions to the duties of a clerkship, received this mass of material from the President and reported it without comment to the House of Representatives, where, as we have seen, it was promptly tabled.

The investigation by Congress into the transactions of the President with Colonel Lane was now at an end. At the next session of the House of Representatives, it would be remarked that the evidence was incomplete; the Ingham committee had neither inquired for nor collected any contradictory testimony to rebut that which the President himself had brought forward. But the friends of Monroe, from whom these objections proceeded, were not trying to reopen the inquiry. As we shall presently relate, they were merely trying to transfer the continuing investigation of Monroe's claims *against* the government from one committee to another. They succeeded, but to the surprise of no one, the favored committee, in its investigations, took no notice of the suggestion, previously made to the prejudice of Monroe, that in the disbursement of public moneys he had misapplied them. It sought only to ascertain the nature and extent of his claims against the government; and in its report it pronounced only upon their intrinsic justice.

Monroe, too, was satisfied to let sleeping dogs lie. He had given a full and honorable explanation of his alleged embezzlements of the public money. He had invited investigation. If Congress had not accepted his invitation, the very omission was a proof of their confidence in the unblemished purity of his private character. One matter was, indeed, unsettled. He had postponed the final adjustment of the furniture account until Congress should have approved the transaction in which he was both buyer and seller. But Congress had expressed no opinion on this point. Taking silence for consent, Monroe asked no further mark of its sentiments. He left the furniture that he had sold to the government in the White House and the money for it in his pocket.

Here we must leave this ancient scandal. We may regret, as historians, that the Ingham committee was limited by its instructions to the taking of ex parte statements and was forbidden to express an opinion on them. We may lament, as respecters of the presidential office, the necessity for an exposure of domestic and household concerns which, in the words of John Quincy Adams, was "almost as incongruous to the station of a President of the United States as it would be to a blooming virgin to exhibit herself naked before a multitude." [25] But we can hardly think that a fuller and more decent investigation would have brought to light any new facts. A court of honor might have criticized the President for his choice of an agent, or gently chided him for imprudence and inattention in money matters, but it could never have held that because Lane had received and embezzled public money, and because he had acted as Monroe's agent in public and in private business, Monroe himself must have known of the embezzlement and been responsible for it. Be that as it may, the President's memoir served its purpose. The doubts of the public were dissolved in the gratification of its curiosity, and the charges of malversation breathed against him by his enemies were silently withdrawn.

III

The Two Missions

Having disposed of the claims of the public on Monroe, we may turn to the claims of Monroe on the public. They consisted in 1825 of balances that he considered due him for his two missions to Europe. Monroe's biographers have generally characterized these claims as *just* and have criticized Congress for raising *obscure objections* to their payment, for *delaying decision,* and for *granting too little* in the end. But these pronouncements seem rather to reflect Monroe's own views than to be grounded on any understanding of the principles which governed the payment of the expenses of foreign missions or of the mode in which those principles had been applied in the settlement of Monroe's particular accounts.[1]

If we are to form any correct idea of the nature of Monroe's claims, let alone pass any judgment on their merits, we must take a preliminary view of Monroe's financial transactions with the public from the day of his ap-

pointment in 1794 as minister plenipotentionary to France
until December 18, 1816, the day on which, by the repayment of a small sum into the treasury of the United States,
he cleared his name from the register of public debtors. We
must ascertain the pecuniary conditions on which, in 1794
and 1803, he consented to serve his country in posts that
would take him from home for nearly eight years; we must
notice, in respect of his second mission, the modifications in
those pecuniary conditions made by President Jefferson in
1804; and we must examine with meticulous care the degree
of lenity or severity with which Monroe was held to his
contract by the Executive Department of the government
in the two settlements of his accounts. Descending into
detail, we must look at the debit and credit sides of those
accounts, that is to say, on the one side at the amounts
drawn from the public Treasury or from the bankers of the
United States at Amsterdam and London, and on the other
at the amounts allowed him by the government under the
various heads of disbursement appropriate to the accounts
of a public minister.

Monroe's first mission began in 1794, when, at the age of
thirty-six, he was sent to France by President Washington
as minister plenipotentiary, in place of Gouverneur Morris,
with instructions to declare and vindicate the neutrality of
the United States in the contest between France and England. The honor was high, and the promised remuneration
might seem not unattractive. Monroe was to receive the
maximum compensation to a public minister permitted by
law. To cover his personal services and all the ordinary

expenses of his mission, he would be allowed a salary at the rate of $9,000 per annum.[2] To defray the extraordinary expenses attendant upon his removal from home, his voyage abroad, and his establishment at Paris, he would be allowed a lump sum of $9,000, technically called an outfit. He could also look forward to a payment at the end of his mission of a quarter's salary, $2,250, to cover the expenses of his return to Albemarle County, Virginia. An allowance, at the rate of $1,350 per annum, would be made to him for the salary of a Secretary of Legation. And upon the production of vouchers or other proofs of payment, he would be reimbursed for such contingent expenses as were not strictly chargeable to salary or outfit.

Accepting these conditions of service, Monroe drew his outfit from the Treasury, sailed with his family from Baltimore on June 18, and reached Paris on August 2. There his financial troubles began. Anxious for the success of his mission but in no position either to threaten or bribe the French, he decided to entertain them. Purchasing a house of extravagant design, he widely extended his hospitality, taking care that the style of it should satisfy those accustomed to good society. One of his parties might have astonished Lucullus. On July 4, 1795, Monroe invited to his house all the Americans in Paris, the ministers of foreign powers, and all the more important members of the French government, army, and navy. The assemblage being too numerous to entertain within doors, he borrowed twelve marquees from the Minister of War and arranged them on a terrace. There the multitude dined—nearly two hundred persons at a single table. After a sumptuous meal and the drinking of many toasts, the entertainment ended with a song: "Où peut-on être mieux qu'au sein de sa famille!" [3] The party was a great success, but music, food, and wine came high and all such extravagancies must press upon his private purse. Years later, in a memorandum written in the third person for the use or information of a friend, Monroe declared that he had spent not only all his salary on his office but more; if he had been richer, he would have spent yet more.[4] As a direct consequence of these expenditures, he contracted debts that would plague him for years to come.

In 1796, Monroe was dismissed from office by President Washington for incompetence, remissness in duty, and the pursuit of wrong courses.[5] In particular, he was blamed for his initial address to the French National Convention and for a later note to the Committee of Public Safety. In the former he had expressed a clear wish for a French victory in the war with England. In the latter he had assured the French government that if it wished to continue its violations of the treaty of commerce with the United States, the American government and people would bear the injury not only with patience but with pleasure.

Monroe received notice of his letter of recall on or about November 10, and the letter itself, on December 6. He took formal leave of the French government on December 30; but he did not immediately return to America. Unwilling to expose himself and his family to the danger and inconvenience of a winter voyage, he notified his friends, but neither President Washington nor Secretary of State Timothy Pickering, that he would postpone his departure until spring; in the interim he would take a trip into Holland with Mrs. Monroe. He put his plans into execution, so that it was not until April 20, 1797, that he sailed from France nor until June 27 that he reached Philadelphia. In the meanwhile John Adams had succeeded Washington as President of the United States.

Once back in America it was incumbent on Monroe to show that he had applied to public purposes the very considerable sums of public money that had passed through his hands. His first occupation, however, was not to settle his accounts with the public but to prepare for publication his famous, or infamous, book against Washington. It was not, therefore, until the end of December that he turned his mind from the business of vindicating his public conduct to that of justifying his use of public money.

At the Treasury the debit side of Monroe's account was known. The records of the State Department showed that Edmund Randolph had furnished him with $10,505 before he left America; the accounts sent in by the bankers of the United States at Amsterdam indicated that he had drawn from them, between September 28, 1794, and February 7, 1797, sums amounting in the aggregate to $34,818.71.[6] These advances or payments were, in the ordinary routine of business, entered, as they became known, on the debit side of Monroe's general account current. Not all of them, however, were strictly chargeable to his mission. Out of the grand total of $45,323.71, the sum of $6,000 had been remitted to him for the relief of Mme. de La Fayette, and $1,505 had been advanced to him for the purchase of books and other articles for the War Department. In a sense, therefore, Monroe had three accounts, rather than one, to settle with the Treasury.

On the discharge side, Monroe's account was blank. It was the rule of office at the Treasury that no credit entries should be made in an account except upon the representations of the accountant. It was up to Monroe, if he wished to lessen or extinguish the balance of more than $45,000 standing against him, to state the credits to which he considered himself entitled under such heads as salary, outfit, returning home, and contingent expenses.

Monroe's disbursements from the fund appropriated for the relief of Mme. de La Fayette are hard to follow because the editor of his writings has not correctly distinguished dollars from pounds from livres.[7] At the Treasury Monroe had two difficulties: he could remember but not prove a payment of 150 pounds sterling to Mme. de La Fayette's agents, and he could prove but not remember a payment of 3,000 gold livres for which he had her receipt. Both items were admitted to his credit. On July 23, 1798, in a settlement of his general account current, he was allowed $4,856.17 for his payments to Mme. de La Fayette[8]—the equivalent in dollars of 53,800 livres in assignats, 3,000 gold livres, and 650 pounds sterling. A subsequent allowance brought the total to $5,509.57.

If the reader wonders why Monroe had not paid out the whole sum voted by Congress for the relief of Mme. de

La Fayette, the following explanation must satisfy him. At an early stage of the proceedings, Alexandre-Marie-François-de-Sales-Théodule, Marquis de Grammont, had advanced 9,000 livres ($1,633.50) to his wife's sister, upon an understanding that Monroe would pay him back when the money from the congressional grant was received. Monroe had given him his personal note for the advance. Accordingly, when the money came, Monroe pocketed 9,000 livres to take up his note. Grammont, however, notified him that he no longer wished reimbursement. Monroe, therefore, paid part of the sum he had deducted to Mme. de La Fayette's agents, but left Paris with a small balance still unpaid.

In settling his War Department account Monroe was troubled by his inability to produce vouchers for more than 298 livres ($54.09) of his disbursements.[9] We may presume that the difficulty was removed by an affidavit and a detailed list of expenditures, for in the end Monroe was allowed $1,435.64.

These allowances were acceptable to Monroe. The settlement of his main account was not, however, accomplished to his satisfaction. After the lapse of more than a quarter of a century, Monroe explained its course as follows: "My account for this mission was settled in my absence, by my friend Mr. Dawson [John Dawson, Representative from Virginia], and a general idea of my instructions to him, as to the conditions of the settlement, is all that I can recollect respecting it, which were, in consideration of my then relation to the Administration, and the difficulties I had to encounter, to make none as to money.

Other cares and duties then pressed on me, compared with which, money weighed as nothing, in the opposite scale." [10]

This statement was, however, not correct, either in its relation of facts or in the inferences that it invited. Anyone reading it in conjunction with his assertion that justice had been denied him, might suppose that the Secretary of State, who determined the principles of settlement, or the accounting officers of the Treasury, who applied those principles to the facts of particular cases, had disallowed, in whole or in part, a number of credits claimed by Monroe, and that Dawson by instruction had tamely acquiesced in the rejections or reductions. But the record tells a different story. With the exception of a single item, amounting to $641.09, Monroe's claims were admitted in full. And with respect to that item, Monroe himself fiercely, and by means that some might consider improper, contested the views of Secretary Pickering.

This dispute had to do with his claim to salary. In justifying his drafts upon the bankers at Amsterdam under this head of expense, Monroe had stated that his service had begun on May 28, 1794, and ended on January 1, 1797. The State Department challenged both these assumptions, holding that his period of service had begun on May 30, 1794, the day on which his pay as member of the Senate ceased, and had ended on December 6, 1796, the day on which he had received his letter of recall. Monroe conceded the first point without difficulty, but not the second. True, he had not performed the functions of a minister after December 6, but he had been ordered to take a formal

leave of the French government, and the Executive Directory had not given him his audience until January 1. The
waiting was at expense, and in some sort of public service;
the public should pay for it.

In support of these ideas, Monroe enlisted the aid of
Thomas Jefferson. Anticipating an unfavorable decision by
the Secretary of State, he armed the Vice President with
arguments and suggested that he mention the affair to
President Adams as coming from himself.[11] When Pickering's views were made known to him, he repeated his solicitations, supplied new arguments, and begged Jefferson to
put them in his own words. He had presented his successor,
General Charles Cotesworth Pinckney, to the Minister of
Foreign Affairs, but he had soon been notified that the
Directory would neither recognize nor receive any minister
from the United States. "Suppose," said Monroe, "that I
had continued to perform the functions of minister, till the
fact was made known to the President and his orders taken,
would the administration have refused to pay me for such
services?" [12]

Monroe, however, in his correspondence with Jefferson,
made one point very clear. He would abide by Pickering's
decision, whatever that decision might be. A disallowance
of his salary for the few weeks in dispute would end his
application. Nor did he wish to be understood as pressing
the allowance. "I only want it placed on its merits to obtain
it if just or according to principle, and, if not, to justify
my supposing it so and drawing the money from the hands
of the bankers in Holland whereby I fall in debt to the
Department of State." [13]

Pickering decided against Monroe, fixing December 6 as the day for stopping his salary. He had no occasion to point out, perhaps he did not know, that Monroe's audience of leave had actually been on December 30, not January 1.[14] Presently the settlement of Monroe's accounts was completed. Apart from this one item, Monroe was allowed everything that he claimed, and even more: outfit, $9,000; salary, $22,647.94; allowance for return, $2,250; contingencies, $399.27; salary of his secretary, $3,397.19;[15] plus an unasked allowance for his secretary's return, $337.50.[16] The reader who has totted up these several credits, not forgetting the allowances on account of Mme. de La Fayette and the War Department, will find that, out of the $45,-323.71 of public money received by Monroe, he had accounted successfully for the application of $44,977.11.

True to his promise, Monroe now abandoned the contest. With silent fury he paid into the Treasury of the United States the small balance of $346.60 found against him.[17] He made no appeal to the equity of Congress. Yet he did not abandon his claim to twenty-six days' additional salary. Careless of the idea that lapse of time or laches might defeat his right, he mentally reserved his demand for presentation at some future day to a tribunal more equitable, or more indulgent, than Secretary Pickering or a Federalist Congress. He could hardly have foreseen that in 1816 he would, in effect, present it to himself.

Monroe's second mission began in 1803, when he was sent to Paris by President Jefferson as envoy extraordinary, to help the resident minister, Robert R. Livingston, in the negotiations that unexpectedly culminated in the Louisiana

Purchase. This mission differed from the first in that Monroe knew from the outset that he would be expected to make financial sacrifices. The remuneration offered him by Jefferson was much less generous than that which he had accepted from Washington; for Jefferson had been elected in 1801 on a promise to reform the prodigalities of his predecessors and to bring the government to a simple and economical course. Monroe was to be a cogent example of the new policy.

All this Jefferson explained to Monroe in a letter dated January 13, 1803. This letter was susceptible of division into two parts. In the first, which Monroe would later publish and republish, Jefferson explained the objects and the urgency of the mission and declared that there could not be two opinions as to the person best qualified to undertake it. There are some men, he announced with gratifying rhetoric, who are born for the public: "Nature, by fitting them for the service of the human race on a broad scale, has stamped them with the evidences of her destination and their duty."

In the second part of this letter, which Monroe never asked permission to publish, Jefferson set out the policy of his Administration with respect to the compensation of special missions and informed Monroe of the manner in which that policy would be applied to his particular case. After complaining that Washington and Adams, in order to increase expense, debt, taxation, and patronage, had tried always to give as much as possible, he stripped the sugar coating from the bitter pill: "The outfit given to ministers resident to enable them to furnish their house, but given by no nation to a temporary minister, who is never expected to take a house or to entertain, but considered on a footing of a voyageur, they gave to their extraordinary missionaries by wholesale. In the beginning of our administration, among other articles of reformation in expense, it was determined not to give an outfit to missionaries extraordinary, and not to incur the expense with any minister of sending a frigate to carry him or bring him. . . . The allowance therefore will be in this and all similar cases, all the expenses of your journey and voyage, taking a ship's cabin to yourself, $9,000 a year from your leaving home till the proceedings of your mission are terminated, and then the quarter's salary for the expenses of the return as prescribed by law." Jefferson ended by pressing Monroe to accept the appointment on the conditions proposed, and to hasten the time of his going. He would receive in Washington what advance he might choose.[18]

Impressed by the urgency of this request, Monroe at once consented to sacrifice his private career to the public good, drew $9,000, the precise amount of the outfit that had been denied him, from the Treasury as an advance to cover his immediate expenses, and proceeded with all deliberate speed to New York, where, early in March, he embarked, with his family, on the *Richmond*, bound for Le Havre.

In Paris he soon had cause to regret his situation. The Court of France, perhaps at all times the most brilliant in Europe, was in 1803, under the Consulate, more than usually so. A minister who would maintain the credit of his country and avoid the charge of disrespect to a foreign government must adapt his exterior style and manners to those of the public functionaries with whom he was associated. Other nations, knowing the expense attending the presentations of their ministers at foreign courts, generally made presents to their families of the most costly, though the most useless, of the articles required. The value of these presents might be estimated at a sum equal to two or three of the American outfits, but Monroe had not been granted even one. In these circumstances, unwilling to attract notice or excite ridicule, Monroe purchased for himself and his wife such articles as were commonly worn by persons of distinction and permitted the charge to fall upon his private fortune.[19]

Monroe's business in France was soon finished, the decision to cede Louisiana having been taken by the First Consul four days before his arrival in Paris.[20] But he had also in his pocket a commission associating him, as minister plenipotentiary and extraordinary, with Charles Pinckney, the resident minister to Spain. For a time, therefore, he contemplated going to Madrid to treat with the Spanish government for the cession of the Floridas, one of the original objects of his double mission. From this course he was dissuaded by Napoleon, who told him that this was not the proper time to go to Spain; that she complained much of the cession which he, Napoleon, had made of Louisiana; and that he must have time to reconcile her to it.

Presently, Monroe learned that, on April 18, his commission had been extended by Jefferson to include not only France and Spain but England. Knowing that Rufus King had left London without nominating a person to take charge of American affairs until the arrival of his successor, he concluded that his best course was to go to London as minister extraordinary and to await further orders in regard to his Spanish mission. Accordingly he crossed the Channel and notified Lord Hawkesbury of his arrival in London on July 20.

No sooner was Monroe established at his new post than he began to bombard the President and the Secretary of State with requests for increased compensation. Apparently regarding his English mission as a way-stop on the route to Madrid, he suggested that the original conditions of his service be revised. Instead of travel expenses, he thought that he might be allowed a half-outfit ($4,500) to Paris and another half-outfit to Madrid or, alternatively, a half-outfit to Paris and his actual expenses to Madrid.[21]

These requests did not fall on deaf ears. There would be a difficulty, Madison told him, in varying the provision made beyond the annual allowance as minister extraordinary to Paris, it being fixed and recorded; but he had now been appointed resident minister in England and an outfit of $9,000 for that mission would be granted as a matter of course.[22] Jefferson made an even more comforting suggestion. He would send him, while still minister to England, on a special mission to Spain with authority to remain there as long as Monroe wanted; his expenses on this special mission would be paid by the government; during his absence he could suspend expense in England and apply his salary to the clearing off of his debts. "We wish to do everything for you which law and rule will permit. But more than this would injure you as much as us." [23]

Monroe's financial position, insofar as it depended on his remuneration from the public, was now greatly improved. An allowance of $9,000 for merely crossing the Channel might be expected to yield him a handsome profit. The grant of *all* the expenses of his Spanish mission, though it would put him to the trouble of keeping an account and preserving vouchers, must prove more remunerative than an allowance of half an outfit or of his travel and contingent expenses only.

Taking advantage of the discretion given him, Monroe closed his residence at London in October 1804 and departed, with his family, for Madrid by way of Paris. At Paris he and his wife were presented at Court and attended the coronation, two functions that required a heavy outlay of public money. In December he left for Madrid, taking along only his secretary; his wife and family he placed, at his own charge, with the family of Fulwar Skipwith in Paris. In June 1805 he returned to Paris, remained there a few weeks, and then, with his family, recrossed the Channel.

Monroe reached England in July 1805, intending to return at once to the United States. Circumstances, however, prevented the realization of his private wishes. Discovering that during his absence from London the relations of England and America had gone from bad to worse, he felt it his duty to stay at his post until a more favorable state of affairs should permit his return. Expecting the moment of his departure from month to month, he remained in London for two years and four months at great expense to himself in such items as house rent, the hire of servants, and the purchase of wine; for, as he himself very truthfully remarked, there is a great difference in the price of living between an establishment formed with a view to some duration and one, in its nature temporary, which is prolonged from time to time by circumstances.[24] It was not until November 15, 1807, that he was able to bring his mission to a close.

From the standpoint of his personal finances, this second part of his English mission was disastrous to Monroe. Not only had he been subjected to an extraordinary expense for the maintenance of a temporary establishment in London, but he had lived in every way beyond his income. Heedless of Jefferson's admonitions to avoid expensive hospitality, he had allowed himself and his wife to be drawn into the most expensive society and subjected "to the interchange of those civilities which were shewn to our public character, and which it would have been dishonorable to our country, as well as to ourselves, not to have returned."[25] In 1828, John Quincy Adams told Governor James Barbour of Virginia that, in his belief, "the debt hanging so heavily upon the old age of Mr. Monroe was chiefly contracted by the expensive establishment of his household in London after his return from Spain in 1805." Barbour replied that Monroe "still owed a large debt to the house of Baring, which he was utterly unable to pay." [26]

There was also his brother Joseph, vain and ostentatious, knowing nothing of money, but always ready to squander it with childish profusion. According to George Hay, if the happiness of Joseph Monroe and his family depended, in any degree, on his skill, or industry in the management of property, or on his capacity to do well any one earthly thing, in that degree they must be wretched: "He is so helpless, so utterly and irremediably good for nothing, such a heavy and overwhelming weight on every body about him, that I never allow myself to think of him." [27] In later years Eliza Monroe (Mrs. George Hay) would attribute her father's embarrassments to the payment of much money for her stylish uncle in London—say 2,000 pounds sterling.[28]

Monroe reached Norfolk in the American ship *Augustus* on December 13, 1807, and proceeded immediately to Washington, where he soon made it clear that painful impressions had been made on his mind during his English mission. He had been insulted in his private character by the appointment in 1806 of William Pinkney as his adjunct in that mission; he had been injured in his political character by the refusal of Jefferson to support the treaty which he and Pinkney had negotiated with England or even to submit it to the Senate. The unanimous vote of the Senate on Pinkney's nomination might seem an endorsement of the views of Dr. George Logan and others, that the important business of a treaty ought not to be entrusted to so feeble and improper a man as Monroe—a minister who was running from London to Paris, from Paris to Madrid, and from thence to London again, but who in fact was not resident anywhere.[29] As for Jefferson and the treaty, Washington had supported Jay in similar circumstances; why had Jefferson done less?

Presently Monroe returned from Washington to Albemarle, where he contemplated publishing a book against Jefferson like that which he had formerly published against Washington. For a number of reasons, however, the most prominent of which was the fear of failure,[30] he gave up the idea and contented himself with writing a public letter of vindication to Madison [31] and with setting himself up as a candidate for the Presidency in opposition to the latter. With respect to the accounts of his mission, he did nothing at all. Feeling that if justice were done him, he would owe the government nothing, but anticipating that he would in fact be found a debtor to the government, he allowed himself to stand charged on the Treasury books for more than $80,000, the whole of the debit side of his account. In 1810 he attributed to his delicacy an omission of duty that others might have imputed to a meaner motive: "I did not mention the subject when at Washington on account of the relation which subsisted then between the administration and me. The same reason has prevented it since." [32]

Whether Monroe would ever have moved to settle his accounts is a question upon which the reader may form his own opinion. The accidental operation of a law of Congress soon left him no option. On March 3, 1809, the last day of Jefferson's Administration, that body, seeking

to ensure a more regular and punctual adjustment of the
accounts of public agents and a prompter payment of the
balances found due, had passed an act requiring the Comptroller of the Treasury to lay before it annually a statement of the public accounts which might have remained
more than three years unsettled or on which balances might
appear to have been due for more than three years. In
February 1810, Monroe read in a Boston paper, sent him
by some kind friend, that the Comptroller, in his first report under this act, had published him to the world as an
apparent debtor to the United States in the sum of $81,-
555.63. A few days later he received a polite note from the
Comptroller himself, Gabriel Duvall, asking him to trans-
mit to the Treasury his accounts of the application and
expenditure of this sum.[33]

Seized by indignation and half-suspecting that the handsome compliment of reporting him as a public defaulter had
originated in the machinations of Madison and his political
supporters, Monroe listened to the advice of his old friend
John Taylor of Caroline, not to remain silent but to bring
the war to the enemy's camp.[34] After a curt exchange of
notes with Duvall [35] and a request to Richard Brent, the
very idle and very drunken Senator from Virginia,[36] to
obtain information for him at the Treasury, he mounted
his horse and rode, though in a wretched state of health,
from his farm in Albemarle County to Washington.

Greatly to his surprise, the reception given him at Washington by President Madison and the officers under him
was kind and friendly, and presently he was able to report

to John Taylor that he had experienced a just and fair conduct in relation to the object which had carried him there.[37] In fact he had secured a second revision of the terms of his employment and a relaxation in the rules of office governing the allowance of contingent expenses.

The debit side of Monroe's account consisted of the sums furnished him from the Treasury at Washington and from the bankers of the United States at Amsterdam and London. These were found to amount in the aggregate to $83,494.46. On the credit side he was allowed without difficulty his salary from January 12, 1803, to November 15, 1807, $43,598.63; his contingent expenses for the French mission, $546.66; his outfit to England, $9,000; the whole expenses of his Spanish mission including his expenses in Paris on the way to and from Madrid, $11,744.83; the allowance for his return, $2,250; and some miscellaneous items, $1,502.88. There remained for consideration the payment of his expenses to Paris at the beginning of his mission; the allowance for his contingent expenses in England; and a claim for compensation, which Monroe now put in, for the extraordinary expenses attending his detention in England after his return from Spain.

Monroe's expenses to Paris had in fact amounted to $2,300, but he now insisted that he ought to have been allowed a full outfit in lieu of expenses. It was all very well that in 1803 Jefferson should have commenced a system of economy; but that system had been discontinued immediately after its application to himself; it was unjust that he should be the only sufferer. These arguments were effective, and Monroe was given credit for an outfit of $9,000 for his mission to France.

The question of his contingent expenses in England proved more troublesome. Unable to prove the whole of his disbursements by vouchers, he asked credit for a sum proportionate to that allowed his predecessor, Rufus King, for the same objects. Finding, however, that the Secretary of State, Robert Smith, was unwilling to allow him $7,539 on vouchers authorizing a credit of not more than $3,650, he, of his own accord, struck from his request the sum of $2,000 and graciously accepted a credit of $5,539.

He was disappointed only in the item claimed on account of his detention in England. By order of President Madison, who perhaps regarded it as cognizable only by the Legislative Branch, it was reserved for further consideration. Monroe had not indicated its amount.

These several allowances were almost sufficient to extinguish the whole of the debit side of Monroe's account. Instead of being found a public debtor in the sum of $8,000 or $9,000, as he might have been under a more rigorous rule of settlement, he was found to owe the United States only $712.46. Monroe returned to Albemarle in a happy frame of mind, reconciled to all appearances with Madison, and ready to rejoin with zeal his old friends.[38]

He did not, however, immediately pay into the Treasury the balance that had been found against him. Instead, on December 17, 1810, he wrote two letters to Secretary Smith designed to show that, in his own view, he was a public creditor.[39] In the first, he recited the circumstances on which his claim for extra expenses in England was founded; considered the question of whether his demands ought to be confined to the increased price in such articles as house rent, the wages of servants, and the hire of horses; and suggested a principle, or precedent, upon which an allowance might lawfully be made to him, to wit, the allowance for demurrage made to Rufus King for the detention of the ship *John Morgan* on which in 1803 he had returned home. In the second letter, he adverted to the closed accounts of his first mission. A mistake, he said, had been made in their adjustment. He had been credited by his salary only to December 6, 1796, the day on which he had received his letter of recall; but he should have been credited to January 1, 1797, the day on which he had had his final audience of leave. The amount due him for twenty-six days of service was $641.09; his right to it was too obvious to require any argument in its support.

The attentive reader will have noticed that in this second letter Monroe was neither entirely accurate nor entirely candid. By placing his audience of leave on January 1 instead of on December 30, he repeated a mistake originally immaterial but which now increased by two the number of days for which he might receive additional salary. By omitting to mention that his demand for additional salary had been formally considered and rejected by the proper authorities at a time when all the facts were still fresh in memory, he permitted or invited the inference that he was the innocent victim of some clerical error rather than the aggrieved loser in a case that had been judged upon its merits.

Secretary Smith, who may well have felt that he had done enough for Monroe, took no action on either of these letters. A few months later Monroe succeeded to his office. As Secretary of State, Monroe found himself in no position immediately to take up or decide upon his own claims. Apart from the considerations of delicacy that naturally presented themselves to his mind, the circumstances surrounding the confirmation of his appointment by the Senate might have suggested to him the advisability of leaving his claims in abeyance.

Monroe had not been confirmed without a struggle. William B. Giles, his former friend, now a Senator from Virginia, had raised an opposition to his appointment founded on a supposed favoritism in the recent settlement of his accounts; Monroe's nomination had been referred to a committee of which Giles was the chairman; his accounts and vouchers had been called for, and a sifting examination made of the settlement. True, the committee had returned a unanimous report in his favor, and Giles himself, under compulsion, had stood up in the Senate and declared himself satisfied with the allowance of the most questionable item, the outfit to Paris. But the language of the report was equivocal and might have conveyed to Monroe a silent warning not to press his luck too far.[40]

For the time being, therefore, Monroe permitted his claims to rest. But the general satisfaction that he had felt with their settlement in 1810 seems rapidly to have evaporated. In 1813 he prepared a memoir, the prototype, as we may suppose, of that which he would present to the Ingham committee in 1825, in which he exhibited the grounds upon which the accounts of his two missions, or at least of his second mission, had been allowed, and in which he stated the injuries which he conceived himself to have suffered in their settlement. This memoir he sent to John Taylor, who declared it excellent but suggested, among other things, that he add an intimation that he might have made, but did not make, a money job out of his various public employments—a curious ground to allege in support of a claim, however justifiable. With greater propriety, Taylor recommended that Monroe pass this memoir through the accounting officers of the Treasury into the hands of a committee of Congress.[41]

Monroe, however, was not yet ready to invite a legislative interference in his pecuniary affairs. On second thought he decided to suppress his memoir. Again we may attribute his reticence to his political situation. By the doctrine of safe precedents, he was next in line for the Presidency. Any action that would bring before the country the dispute that had agitated the executive council of the Senate in 1810 could only give color to an idea, already widespread, that Monroe in that year had entered into an improper combination with the Administration.

That idea, not confined to Federalists, would be put into words by A. C. Hanson of Maryland in 1814: "The Great Magician [Jefferson] ascended the pinnacle of his favorite mount, and waved his wand over Richmond. It had an electrical effect. The parties were immediately brought to the famous conference at Monticello. All was instantly arranged. The disgraced Minister was reconciled and again taken into favor. His aberrations were pardoned. He returned to Richmond, and there received the requisite *white-washing*, in the modern political mode. He was quickly exalted to the gubernatorial chair of the great State, as a preliminary step to a regular induction to the Office of State, which he now fills. Having sat out the appointed period upon the patent stool of political repentance, he then passed from his probationary state of Governor to his allotted station in the direct line of Virginia succession, and is ere long to mount the throne. Yes, sir, *James the Second* is ripe and ready to undergo the ceremonies of coronation whenever *James the First* shall see fit to abdicate in his favor." [42]

It was not until late in 1816, when the event of the presidential election could no longer be in doubt, that Monroe considered it appropriate to pursue his remedy. On November 1 he addressed a letter to his old companion-in-arms, Joseph Anderson, now Comptroller of the Treasury, in which he noted that for six years his name had been reported annually on the list of public debtors; it was now his intention to pay the balance due. But there were one or two things that the Comptroller should know. He himself had a claim against the government, not strictly within the letter of the law, for his extra expenses in England. According to custom, this claim must be decided by the Secretary of State; his predecessor had admitted its equity but had left it unsettled; he, Monroe, would not settle his own account; it must therefore remain suspended. Then, almost as an afterthought, he came to the point. He presumed there could be no objection to the correction of an error in the settlement of the account of his first mission to France, an error mentioned in his letter of December 17, 1810, to Secretary Smith. He had accidentally been docked of twenty-six days' salary due him for the period of waiting for his audience of leave from the Executive Directory.[43]

The request of an incoming President to a subordinate official is not easily to be distiguished from a command. In a very short time Monroe was gratified to learn that the accounting officers had considered his claim, allowed it, and passed to his credit the sum of $641.09. The Comptroller also offered a conjecture as to the cause of the mistake: Pickering must have taken the date of Monroe's letter advising him that he had received his notice of recall as the date on which he had had his audience of leave.[44] This very wrong but agreeable guess Monroe did not feel called on to correct. He filed the Comptroller's letter for future use, paid off the trifling balance of $71.36 that still stood against him, and erased his name from the list of public debtors.

From the point of view of the Treasury and the public, the accounts of Monroe's two missions, with the exception of one item unknown to the public, might now be considered finally closed. In 1826, indeed, an examination of the Treasury records was made by the Register of the Treasury for the purpose of stating an account of all claims for allowances made by Monroe upon the government which had been disallowed. Joseph Nourse, who had held the office of Register from the establishment of the government in 1789, could find only one such claim—the item for extra expenses in England suspended in 1810 under the authority of Secretary Smith.[45] To all appearances every other claim urged by Monroe had been allowed in full.

Yet appearances were deceitful. Monroe had several claims, more or less informal, which he meant at an appropriate time, probably upon his final retirement from public office, to present to the public and to prosecute to a final settlement. Still other items of account lay in the back of his mind, to be brought forward first in the form of a disclaimer but finally in the form of an assertion of right. With this second category of unmade claims we shall not for the moment be concerned.

Portrait of James Monroe by Gilbert Stuart. *Courtesy of The Metropolitan Museum of Art, Bequest of Seth Low, 1929.*

(Above) Wash drawing of the White House (4½" x 7⅞") from a sketchbook by George Heriot. His caption reads "Palace of the President 1st July 1815." *Courtesy of The New-York Historical Society, New York City.*

(Below) "Ash Lawn," home of James Monroe near Charlottesville, Virginia. *By Ewing Galloway, N.Y.*

The Green Room in the White House, showing the fireplace mantel installed by President Monroe. *Photo Courtesy National Park Service.*

Purchases made in France for the White House during
Monroe's administration. (Above, left) One of seven dozen
flat plates, part of a dessert service for thirty in porcelain
with a purple border having five vignettes representing
Force, Agriculture, Commerce, the Arts, and the Sciences,
with the arms of the United States in the bowl of the plate.
120 francs per dozen. *The H. F. DuPont Winterthur
Museum, Winterthur, Delaware.* (Above, right) Two richly
decorated porcelain vases depicting Homer and Belisarius,
costing 500 francs. *Photo Courtesy National Park Service.*
(Below) Clock of dull gilt bronze showing Hannibal after
the battle of Cannae, costing 900 francs. Two Etruscan-shaped
vases of dull gilt adorned with flowers, price not itemized.
Photo Courtesy National Park Service.

IV

The Claims of 1825

In the memoir delivered by Monroe to the Ingham committee on January 18, 1825, Monroe undertook to enumerate, explain, and justify his immediate claims. After a preliminary recitation of the high offices that he had held since 1794, he condescended to list the instances in which he thought that justice had been withheld from him. All were connected with his two missions to Europe. He had suffered injury in the settlement of the accounts of his first mission by the premature suspension of his compensation and the insufficient allowance made to him for contingent disbursements. He had suffered injury in the settlement of the accounts of his second mission by the refusal of President Jefferson to allow him, at the time of his appointment, an outfit to Paris; by an omission on his own part to claim reimbursement for a payment of demurrage; by the inadequate allowance made to him for contingent disbursements in England; and by the failure of President Madison to allow him extra compensation for the extraordinary expenses to which he had been subjected in England after his return from Spain. These six injuries, when formed into an account, would produce seven claims.

To delimit the first of these claims, it will be necessary to remind ourselves of a few dates. In 1798, Pickering had allowed Monroe's claim to salary only until December 6, 1796, the day when he had received his letter of recall; but in 1816 Monroe had obtained a continuance of that salary until January 1, 1797, the day upon which, supposedly, he had taken leave of the Executive Directory. Now, in 1825, he asked Congress to continue his salary from January 1, 1797, until April 20, 1797, the day of his embarkation at Bordeaux on a ship bound for Philadelphia. If allowed, this claim must produce $2,750.[1]

At what period Monroe conceived that he ought to be paid the salary of a minister plenipotentiary for the three months and twenty days following the termination of his mission, may not easily be ascertained. It is certain that he made no such claim at the time the accounts of that mission were in the course of settlement at the Treasury; nor had he drawn any money on account of it from the hands of the bankers in Holland; even his private correspondence with Jefferson and Dawson contained no hint that his salary should be continued beyond the date when his recall took effect. But in 1810 he had casually remarked to Secretary Smith that no allowance had ever been made to him for his winter's detention in France and had intimated that if justice were done him, an allowance ought still to be made.

And in 1816, when himself Secretary of State, he had made a more formal representation of this idea. At the end of his letter requesting, or directing, the Comptroller of the Treasury to reopen the closed accounts of his first mission and to continue his salary for an additional twenty-six days, he wrote: "My claim to compensation for the time that I was detained in France after my recall, (it being in the winter) before I could obtain a passage for myself and family in a ship sailing for the United States, it being of a kind usually referred to the head of the Department, will necessarily remain suspended. I mention it merely to show that I do not relinquish the claim."

Now, in 1825, he presented this claim for the consideration of Congress and supported it by argument. His salary account, he conceded, had, though with some delay, been finally settled in accordance with the general rule of the Treasury which terminated the salaries of public ministers at the time of their taking leave of the courts to which they were accredited. But in his case a departure from the general rule would have been amply justified. His situation was unique: "No other example of the kind exists; so that the case depends on its own circumstances, without the aid of precedents." He had been removed from office at a time when he could not, even if he would, return home. For three months and twenty days he had been exposed to an unavoidable expense, for which he had received no allowance. "Had I resigned, or asked my recall, the period at which it would have taken effect would have been arranged in a manner to guard against such inconvenience and loss. It would doubtless have been postponed until the Spring, the time when I did sail. It is unjust that my recall should operate in such manner as to take from me the compensation allowed to the mission, for the term during which I could not sail."

To buttress this argument, Monroe attached to his remarks three documents. Each was signed by a character of great respectability, who was present in Europe at the time, engaged in commerce, and well acquainted with the state of affairs. All were dated September 1824, and all followed a common pattern. Conflated and condensed, they might read as follows: "I have just learned with surprise that no allowance has ever been made to you for the expenses you incurred in consequence of your detention in France after you had your audience of leave of the French Directory in the winter of 1796-97. On recurring to my correspondence I find that owing to the British and French restrictions on our shipping at that period, there were but few American vessels in the French ports, and freights for such were extremely high. I recollect frequently hearing mention made of the serious difficulty you labored under to find a suitable vessel to take your family home at that inclement season." [2]

To prove that his claim was not entirely new, Monroe produced two letters or reports from the accounting officers of the Treasury, dated November 1816.[3] One, from Comptroller Anderson, quoted verbatim Monroe's own statement of the claim. Anderson had thought it proper to make the extract "in order that a full view of your claim, as stated, may be preserved upon the books of this office, as it appears, at present, for the reasons which you have offered, entirely uncertain at what period a final adjustment and settlement of your account with the United States will be made." The other, from Stephen Pleasonton, Fifth Auditor of the Treasury, tended to show that if, in 1816, Monroe had permitted the settlement of his claim, the accounting officers would have allowed it; for in fulsome language Pleasonton pronounced it fair and well founded: "If justice were done him, his salary would be continued to the 20th of April, 1797, previous to which it was not in his power to leave France with his family, without incurring the dangers and hardships of a winter passage." Besides proving the existence of the claim and Monroe's intention to preserve it, these letters might be useful, were the accounting officers ever to be called upon by Congress to express an opinion on its equity; for in 1825 Anderson and Pleasonton were still in office and they would remain there until 1836 and 1855, respectively.

These explanations and evidences might, in the partial view of a select committee, incline the scales of justice in favor of Monroe. In the pan against him lay the principle by which his salary account had actually been settled—that of allowing compensation to ministers only to the time of their audience of leave. In the other pan lay a practice that in Monroe's case, and in his case alone, had been abrogated—that of permitting a minister to choose his own time of taking leave. Granted that the public service might be deemed to require his sudden recall, without regard to the season or the circumstances which might prevent him from returning within the usual time, that fact ought not to deprive him of his salary as well as his office. An allowance of this item would not only be just but in accordance with the spirit of the established usage of the government.

The historian, however, may find in the premises of Monroe's argument some erroneous relations of fact; the moralist, some evidences of deliberate deception. It is somewhat remarkable that Monroe should have insisted on the singularity of his case; for there were in fact two precedents that might seem to have some bearing on it. Oliver Ellsworth and John Armstrong had both been ministers to France; each had claimed salary for the period between his taking leave of the French Court and his embarkation for home; Ellsworth's claim had been rejected, but Armstrong's had been allowed.[4] Neither of these precedents, however, though they might seem to be of opposite tendencies, could help Monroe. Ellsworth had asked compensation on the ground that he was detained in France by sickness; Secretary Madison had refused it on the ground that only Congress could suffer equitable considerations to influence a departure from the general rule. A reference to this case would only show that Monroe had not been treated differently from other ministers by the Executive; it might also suggest that his remedy in Congress was barred by laches of the claimant and lapse of time.

Armstrong, on the other hand, had asked compensation on the ground that he had opened a correspondence with William Pinkney, the minister at London, in relation to the repeal of the British Orders in Council and Napoleon's Berlin and Milan Decrees, and that it was important that he should await the result at Bordeaux; the Secretary of State, Monroe himself, had admitted the force of these pleadings and had allowed the claim. A reference to a precedent of his own manufacture might expose Monroe to criticism. Besides, it could only call attention to the difference in the situation of a disgraced minister traveling in Holland for his private pleasure and that of an undisgraced minister waiting at Bordeaux on public business.

Whether Monroe can justly be blamed for pretending that his claim was unique, is a question upon which philosophers may rationally dispute. Only an incurable casuist, however, could justify the deceptions and evasions by which he sought to show that his detention in Europe was not voluntary but compulsive. "The fact is, that I did not, and could not, leave France before the 20th of April," he wrote to the Ingham committee, and supported the declaration with vouchers suggesting or asserting that he had tried and failed to obtain a winter passage. But the record tells another story. On January 8, 1797, he informed a correspondent in America that he had no intention of leaving Europe until April and that he meant to view Holland in the interim.[5] In 1826 he would state his actual movements: "A few days after I took my leave of the Directory . . . I proceeded to Holland and remained there till the Spring, at which time I hurried through France to Bordeaux, from which port we sailed." [6] Even his memoir to the Ingham committee contained a virtual admission that he had made no effort to obtain a passage: "I believe the fact to be, that, had I been willing to encounter a winter's passage, with my family, I could not have procured a vessel to bring me home."

By including this sentence in his observations Monroe might protect himself from a charge of perverting the facts. By putting it in a subjunctive form he might hope to conceal its real meaning. A simple declaratory statement of the truth would have destroyed his case. A member of Congress, one of the very best, would make such a statement in 1831 long after the claim had been allowed: "By order of the President of the United States, his diplomatic functions ceased on the 1st of January. He was bound to obey that order, and could not prolong the term of service beyond the period fixed by his Government. As a minister, no intercourse with France was entertained by him subsequently to this time, and the United States derived not a single advantage from his delay in returning home. It must then be considered as a measure adopted by Mr. Monroe, from a regard to his own private convenience or personal accommodation, with which the public has nothing to do. . . . From no part of the evidence adduced, can I discover that he ever made one effort to obtain a passage between the 1st of January and 20th of April, 1797; on the contrary. . . . Then all the reasons assigned for the delay, such as the war in Europe, the disturbed state of our commerce, the blockade of the French coast, etc., etc., amount to nothing; for, let those difficulties be what they might, no attempt to surmount or overcome them appears to have been made; and the detention must be regarded as his own voluntary act." [7]

But what if Monroe had stated his case in a frank and truthful way? It would have been clear that he was asking Congress to extend his pay for nearly four months because he had not chosen to cross the Atlantic at an inclement season. And would Congress have been likely to grant his request? Even as he made it, in January 1825, numerous vessels were arriving from Europe in the ordinary course of commerce; and it might have been remembered that he himself had voluntarily taken a winter passage from England in 1807.

Another portion of Monroe's argument—that his recall had been unasked—while literally true, might also be sophistical. For to force one's own recall is not very different from asking it, insofar as the date of its taking effect may be concerned. In the summer of 1796, Monroe had told a private correspondent that he would demand his recall, "did I not wish rather to be recalled than to demand it." [8] And in his public book against Washington he had flatly stated that he had long considered his recall probable—"which compulsory mode of retreat I preferred to a voluntary one." [9] Washington, it is true, had laughed at this final assertion—"Curious and laughable to hear a man under his circumstances talking serious in this stile when his recall was a second death to him" [10]—but Monroe's actions, public and private, gave it some color of probable truth. Indeed, as a prudent man, Monroe might have expected his dismissal a year before it took place. In June

1795, he had "laid a plot for blowing up the administration" by attacking it anonymously in Bache's paper.[11] The premature discovery of this plot must, by the unchanging laws of politics, have led to his removal—as indeed it eventually did.

The second item in Monroe's account had to do with the amount allowed him in 1799 for the contingent expenses of his first mission. No minister, he insisted, had ever been used as an agent by every American citizen in France; his house had been daily filled by the captains and supercargoes of vessels seized and detained in French ports; he had been compelled to employ three or four assistant secretaries, to rent a house for them distinct from his own, and to support them at his own expense. In addition he had made heavy disbursements for newspapers, stationery, postage, presents and gratuities to French officials and citizens, loans and gifts to distressed Americans. And for all this what had he been allowed in the settlement of his accounts? Seventy livres for newspapers sent to the Department of State, 340 livres for postage, 200 livres for a flag presented to the National Convention—a grand total of $110.71, or, stated at an annual rate, $30.40 per year. The inadequacy of the allowance might be immediately apparent to the members of Congress if they would examine a statement of the contingent expenses allowed to every foreign minister under the present government, commencing with Mr. Gouverneur Morris in France and General Thomas Pinckney in England, down to the present time. He had procured such a statement from the accounting officers of the Treasury, and he now submitted it. It would suggest that, at the very least, he should have been allowed his contingent expenses at the rate of $1,500 a year. From August 1, 1794, to January 1, 1797, was a period of two years and five months; for this period he should have been allowed $3,625; he had actually been allowed $110; the balance due him was $3,515. In conclusion, he modestly noticed that he charged nothing for the three months and twenty days after his recall, during which he had, to a certain extent, been exposed to like contingencies.

As in the instance of his first claim, there are some aspects of this argument that require comment. To begin with, the comparison offered by Monroe between the allowances made to himself and to others was very much rigged in his favor. In these early days the contingent expenses of a foreign mission were defined by usage as the money spent for stationery, postage, newspapers, messengers to carry despatches, and the like.[12] But in addition a minister might expect reimbursement for any extraordinary expenses to which he might be subjected. In stating the allowances made to him for contingencies, Monroe omitted of course the credits granted to him for his payments to Mme. de La Fayette ($5,509.57) and for his purchase of a military library ($1,435.64), but he omitted also some items that might seem to have come within even the narrowest definition of contingencies.[13] In stating the allowances made to others, he was not so careful to discriminate contingent from extraordinary expenses. Nor did he candidly admit the crudity of his tables. When, for example, he pointed to the large allowances made to John Jay, the alphabetical envoy, as he sometimes called him, he might well have remarked that Jay had been allowed the full expenses of his mission, plus his salary as Chief Justice ($4,000), in lieu of the outfit, salary, and other allowances of a minister plenipotentiary; had he done so, however, he would have exposed the absurdity of contrasting the whole expenses of one mission with the incidental expenses of another.

In the second place, Monroe's complaint invited the inference that Secretary Pickering or the accounting officers of the Treasury were to blame for the smallness of the allowance made to him in 1799. Yet the truth was that, in the account which he then presented, the whole charge for contingencies was admitted. Lewis Williams would later remark: "If any other or greater account existed at that time, it was known only to Mr. Monroe, and, as he failed to produce it, the fault was his own. The Government could not be required, by any principle, to settle an account of which it had no knowledge." [14]

In the third place, Monroe, in reciting the heavy expense to which he had been subjected in Paris, failed to point out that the greater part of this expense could not, by the precedents of office, have been allowed him by any executive officer under any head of account. Two years had scarcely passed since Monroe himself, as President, had rejected a similar claim submitted by General Armstrong. Armstrong had belatedly asked an allowance for some extraordinary expenses to which he had been subjected during his mission to France, but Monroe had coldly replied:

cases. ~~[struck through]~~

~~[struck through]~~

~~[struck through]~~

~~[struck through]~~

~~[struck through]~~

On the second branch of General Armstrong's claim, it
would be equally improper for me to decide. The services
referred to are a proper subject for legislative consideration
and provision. They do not fall within the scope contemplated by the contingent fund appropriated for foreign
intercourse, or it is presumed that the claim would
have been decided, on his return ~~home~~, and on the
settlement of the other items of his account.

                              James Monroe.

Washington
april 10. 1823.

"They do not fall within the scope contemplated by the contingent fund appropriated for foreign intercourse, or, it is presumed that the claim would have been decided on his return home, and on the settlement of the other items of his account." [15]

Monroe's third claim was even more extraordinary. He had, as we have seen, in 1810 persuaded Madison to allow him the outfit to Paris that Jefferson in 1803 had refused him. He now demanded interest on that outfit for the time it had been withheld, that is to say, from January 10, 1803, until April 1, 1810. He suggested no rate but calculated, or miscalculated, the sum due him as $4,455.[16] And he noted, with modest self-applause, that he was asking simple interest only, in a case where compound interest was justly due.

Reserving for future comment the question of the government's legal or moral duty to pay interest on unsettled claims, we may notice some other aspects of this demand. In a wire-drawn argument Monroe explained that the credit allowed by Madison in 1810 must be looked upon as the belated payment of a debt incurred by Jefferson in 1803. The delay had cost him money; had he been given the outfit when it was due, the $9,000 would have been his own and he might have availed himself of it for his private engagements as well as his public duties; without it, he had been compelled to borrow money to put his affairs in order before leaving America, and upon these loans he had paid compound interest; a demand now for simple interest on a debt unpaid for more than seven years could hardly be called unjust.

Passing over the preposterous idea that an allowance refused by Jefferson in 1803 could form the basis for an interest claim in 1810, we need only notice the errors and omissions that characterized Monroe's statement of facts. It was not true that Monroe had suffered in any way from the delay in allowing his outfit. He had taken the amount of an outfit, $9,000, from the Treasury in 1803, only a week after his salary commenced, under the head of an advance for expenses to Paris, and he had never returned the unspent balance; nor had he paid interest on it. The government was never at any time during the continuance of his mission indebted to him for the amount of an outfit. On the settlement of his accounts in 1810 a balance was ascertained to be due from him, after allowing the outfit. His situation in 1810 was consequently precisely the same as if he had been granted an outfit to begin with. The talk about interest was meaningless. His expenses to Paris had come to $2,300; for seven years he had owed the government $6,700. The compound interest that he saved on this sum must offset that to which he might have been liable for his private borrowings of the same amount.

Monroe's fourth claim was for demurrage. On March 5 and 7, 1803, he had paid Isaac Hicks, a sea captain, a total of $350 for a passage from New York to Le Havre on the ship *Warren* but he had been unable to use it, his instructions not having been prepared in time. He had casually omitted this item when his account was settled in 1810. In proof of payment he could produce Hicks' receipt.

Here again Monroe was not quite frank in his explanations. It was doubtless true that he had paid the money and failed to include the payment in his statement of expenses to Paris. But that statement had not been used in the settlement of his accounts. Instead of the expenses promised him, which, according to his own memoranda, amounted to $2,300 (including the payment for his unused passage), he had been allowed an outfit of $9,000, for the disbursement of which no account need be rendered. Had Monroe produced the forgotten voucher in 1810, it might have been considered irrelevant by the accounting officers.

Indeed it is hard to believe that Monroe, in 1810, had forgotten this item. He had studied with care the allowances for contingent expenses made to Rufus King. One of these, demurrage for the ship *John Morgan*, might have reminded him of his own case. That he noticed it is certain, for he mentioned it in another connection in the observations which he furnished to Secretary Smith.[17] One is tempted to think that, in 1810, he considered it as covered by the lump-sum allowance of $9,000 for his outfit to Paris.

Monroe's fifth claim could neither be misrepresented nor misunderstood. In 1810 he had asked the Secretary of State to overlook the absence of vouchers and to allow him $7,539 for the contingent expenses of his mission to England, but in the end he had struck from his demand the sum of $2,000, and accepted an allowance of the balance. Now he asked Congress to restore the sum thus relinquished. With a show of candor, he conceded in a note that, in 1810, he might have overstated the allowance made to Rufus King under this head of expense; if so, he would permit his claim to be recalculated.[18] He did not find it necessary to point out that he had asked an allowance for the whole period of his English mission, four years and four months, although he had been absent from England on an expense account for nearly a year of that time.

Monroe's sixth claim was an iteration of his demand for compensation for the extra expenses to which he had been subjected in England after his return from Spain. This was the claim suspended by President Madison in 1810 and continued in suspension by himself. As we have seen, it was grounded on the idea that the public should reimburse him for the excessive cost of maintaining a temporary establishment in London for two years and four months.

Of all Monroe's claims this was in some respects the most extraordinary. It might seem a singular illustration of Nathaniel Macon's remarks that claims against the government were something like wine and spirits; they improved by age.[19] In 1810, Monroe had not fixed the amount of this claim; in his own statement of account the charge was run out in blank. The omission might be thought fatal to his case, for as a member of Congress would later remark: "He alone knew what these extraordinary expenses were, and it was his duty to ascertain and state them. No officer of Government could be required to guess at the amount, and to pay him according to that uncertain, whimsical mode of doing business."[20] In 1816, in his letter to the

Comptroller of the Treasury, he had mentioned the claim, but again without stating its amount. In 1821, in his letter to the First Auditor, he had been more explicit; he had declared his right to at least half an outfit ($4,500) for his special mission to England in addition to the full outfit to which he was entitled as resident minister. Now, in 1825, he demanded an allowance at the rate of not less than $4,500 a year for the two years and four months of his detention in England. In effect, he asked, that for this period his salary as minister be increased from $9,000 a year, the maximum rate permitted by law, to at least $13,-500.

To support this astonishing claim, the amount of which might be placed at $10,500, Monroe furnished the Ingham committee with a decision made by himself in 1821, in which he had examined all the precedents, as to salaries and outfits, which had been allowed to American ministers in Europe from the commencement of the government until that day.

That this view of the precedents tended to justify Monroe's own claim may perhaps be conceded. But its weight would have been somewhat diminished had Monroe emphasized the fact that he himself was responsible for most of the relevant examples. As Secretary of State, he had frequently been compelled, under the sanction of President Madison, to decide claims analogous to his own. Without hesitation he had performed the embarrassing duty. "Had I not decided," he would later explain to the Comptroller of the Treasury, "great injury might have been the consequence. Public affairs, of the highest importance, might, and probably would, have been suspended, if, in some instances, they had not failed. Bound to decide, I have done it, according to my own judgment, by an impartial, but liberal, construction of the law, with a view to the public welfare." [21] As President, he had acted somewhat differently. Unwilling to leave the decision of claims resembling his own to the severe and parsimonious judgment of John Quincy Adams, his Secretary of State, he had himself taken cognizance of them. If the resemblance was perfect, he suspended them on the ground that a man ought not to be a judge in his own cause; if imperfect, he decided them on their merits. But in every case he included in his decision, by way of comparison, an ample explanation and justification of his own claim and a hint or declaration that the money for his extra expenses in England was "unquestionably due" him.

Two examples may prove instructive. John Armstrong, while minister plenipotentiary of the United States at Paris, had been appointed commissioner plenipotentiary to treat with a minister of Spain at the same place for the adjustment of all differences between the United States and Spain. This extra duty had exposed him for four years to extra cares, labor, and expense. On his return to America in 1810 he had claimed extra compensation, but it had not been allowed. During the Presidency of Monroe he had revived his claim; but Monroe had refused to decide it. In a document dated April 10, 1823, he assimilated Armstrong's demand to his own, pronounced them both just, and then continued: "In comparing my claim with that of General Armstrong, it will be seen that it would be impossible for me to decide on his, without giving an unqualified sanction to my own, so far at least as related to the special mission to England. For this reason I deem it improper to make any decision on its merits." [22] Armstrong was left without his money, but he might take consolation in the thought that his secret enemy had admitted the justice of his petition and might presently use it as a voucher in support of his own just demands.

Henry Clay was more fortunate. In 1821 he preferred, for the first time, a claim for the extraordinary expenses attending his transfer in 1815 from Ghent to London and his negotiation there, jointly with John Quincy Adams and Albert Gallatin, of a commercial treaty with England. Knowing that Adams, now Secretary of State, considered the allowance of this claim to be "contrary to every precedent and every principle," Monroe referred it to himself. In his decision, rendered not without hesitation and difficulty, he compared Clay's claim with his own and perceived a subtle distinction between the two. With Clay, the theater of negotiation was changed; and he, in consequence, was compelled to move, during the whole of the negotiation, in a new and more expensive circle. With himself, the theater of negotiation remained the same, but unforeseen circumstances raised the expenses of his mission to a maximum throughout. Accordingly, setting aside the opinion of Adams and arming himself with a contrary opinion extorted from an unwilling Attorney General, Monroe allowed Clay half an outfit, or $4,500.[23]

Monroe's seventh and last claim was for interest on the capital amount of each of his other claims from the time at which the service upon which it was founded was rendered, till paid. As to the exact day upon which the calculation of interest should commence, each item must speak for itself. Those of the first mission became due: for the contingencies, annually; for the detention in France, on the day he sailed for home. Those of the second mission became due: for the interest on the outfit withheld (converted to a capital sum), on the day the outfit was allowed; for the unused passage to France, on the day he paid Captain Hicks; for the contingencies in England, annually; for the detention in England, annually or on the termination of his mission.[24] Monroe mentioned no rate of interest, but it is fair to assume that he expected 6 per cent. A rough calculation, assuming final payment of the capital sums in December 1825, will fix the amount of his interest claim at about $30,000.

To support this application Monroe argued, in effect: A demand for interest always rests upon grounds identical with those of the debt upon which it is claimed; the admission of interest is, therefore, a necessary consequence of the admission of principal; such was the general rule, too obvious and too well established in transactions between individuals in private life to admit of doubt. To be sure, there were certain contingencies that might prevent the operation of this rule in particular cases. If it could be shown, for example, that the claimant himself was responsible for the failure of the government to make its allowances at the proper times, interest for the period of delay might justifiably be refused. But what had these contingencies to do with Monroe? From whom did the delay proceed? By whom was the injury done? By the government itself. Could the government, then, render justice by paying the principal after withholding it for so long a time?

With regard to the latter part of this argument—that the government was to blame for Monroe's injuries—little comment is needed. It could only be valid if he could show that he had presented his claims at the proper times to the appropriate authorities, Executive or Legislative, as the case might be, and that they had been negligent in considering and deciding them. But this, upon his own showing, he could not do. In his message of January 5, 1825, to Congress he had explained that his claims were not of a type that could be settled by the accounting officers of the Treasury; they could be settled only by Congress. And he had conceded that, out of delicacy, he had never until that moment presented them to Congress. In his letter to the Ingham committee he gave his case away even more completely by admitting that he had never urged his demands upon *any* branch of the government: "I declined pressing my claims on any administration, or even mentioning them, preferring rather to bear the additional injury which I sustained by the delay, or even the entire loss, than to subject either to the responsibility of passing, or the mortification of rejecting, them. I have looked to Congress, as the only tribunal which could with strict propriety decide on them, and to the period of my retirement from this office, as that beyond which there could be no motive for longer delay."

By imputing blame to the public for the nonpayment of claims that he himself had reserved or held back till a more suitable time to present them, Monroe could hardly have helped his cause. Indeed, he might seem to have invited the retort that was actually made to him some years later: "Now if these claims were not paid because Mr. Monroe was in office, is it right he should be allowed interest on that account? The United States did him a favor by keeping him in office, and now, forsooth, we are called upon, as a wrongdoer, to pay interest. The continuance in office, if, in fact, it prevented the settlement of his claims, must be regarded as his own act; otherwise you place the Government in the awkward predicament of being obliged to pay interest on damages, because they had previously done him a favor by keeping him in office." [25]

The first part of Monroe's argument—that, if the principal of a claim is justly due, the payment of interest, in a legal point of view, necessarily follows—deserves more extended comment. Monroe well knew, and concealed his knowledge, that this was *not* the general rule and established practice of the government but its exact opposite. Unless Congress by special words sanctioned the allowance of interest on settled claims, the accounting officers of the Treasury, and for that matter the congressional committees of claims, invariably refused it.

Behind that practice lay a legal presumption fortified by a fear of the practical consequences that would follow the adoption of the rule of private business. "I have said," exclaimed a member of Congress in 1831, "Government does not pay interest on claims. Why should it be so? Because Government is a moral person, always ready and willing to pay its debts. If any citizen is delayed in the payment of his claim, it is because he does not produce it, or does not offer the requisite evidence to sustain it. The fault, then, is his own, and he should not be permitted to take advantage of it, and mulct the Government in damages. If such were the case, individuals who have claims would never bring them forward, because they would constitute a valuable kind of stock, if permitted to draw interest while they had been reserved, or kept back in the hands of the claimants." [26]

That Monroe, in 1825, was ignorant of this rule, cannot be pretended. For in 1824 the demand of Virginia for interest on a settled claim had been considered by the Monroe administration in a full meeting and had been rejected on the ground that the allowance could not be made by the Executive, the uniform decision in such cases having been against it.[27] At this meeting, John Quincy Adams had argued that, if the wise and just precedents that governed the settlement of accounts were once broken in upon in favor of a State, he could discern no principle upon which interest could be denied to individuals.[28] But of all this, Monroe, in his correspondence with the Ingham committee, said nothing. Had he correctly stated the rule governing the allowance of interest on private claims, had he even refrained from misstating it, he would have made it only too clear that, in asking Congress to allow him a few thousand dollars under the head of interest lawfully due, he was asking it to establish a precedent that might swallow hundreds of millions of dollars in the future and countenance untold frauds.

Such were the claims that Monroe in January 1825 presented in a very partial and misleading light to the Ingham committee. Their capital amount came to $23,570; the interest allegedly due on them approached $30,000, and was increasing at the rate of $1,400 a year. If Congress were to act upon them at its December session, the earliest opportunity, an appropriation of more than $53,000 would be needed to discharge them.

V

The Allowances of 1826

The Ingham committee was precluded by its instructions from expressing any opinion on the merits or demerits of Monroe's demands; it could not even investigate the facts, let alone report them. Its functions were merely clerical: it was to hear what the President had to communicate, to report his ex parte statements to the House, and there was to be an end to the business. The report was to be laid on the table, to be acted on at the next Congress.

This arrangement, as we have seen, was a blow to Monroe, who would much have preferred the reference of his explanations to a committee unshackled by instructions, a committee of his friends who would almost certainly render a report in his favor. Nevertheless, a printed document exhibiting his claims in a light of his own choosing might be put to advantage. Congress adjourned March 3, 1825, not to meet again until December 5. During the intervening months Monroe took what precautions he could to strengthen and consolidate his position. Procuring a number of copies of the Ingham committee's report, he circulated them amongst his friends and acquaintances, explaining that he was very anxious that the subject be well understood in all its parts, especially by those for whose good opinion he entertained the highest respect.

In a letter to Andrew Jackson, with whom his relations were for the moment strained, he summarized his case with brevity and perspicacity: "It fell to my lot to suffer under the decision of one party when the contest was at the highest between them and of the other when the sentiment in favor of economy had its greatest force. There never was a time that I could expect, or ask an important decision on the subject, until that of which I availed myself. I wish, as I have stated, nothing but justice, and shall never touch the subject again, if every claim is rejected." [1]

Some of the replies to his letters have been preserved. John Marshall, the Chief Justice, answered politely and sympathetically: "I think you are entitled to receive as much as has ever been allowed to others for similar services and that justice will not be stinted by any implied concession made under circumstances when it could not be withheld" [2]—a gratifying corroboration of Monroe's contention that his acceptance of the appointment by Jefferson to France did not imply an acceptance of the conditions proposed.

The next Congress met in December, and on the nineteenth of that month Monroe's petition was referred by the House of Representatives to the standing Committee of

Claims, a reference that boded ill for its success. Four days later the Committee of Claims asked to be discharged from the further consideration of Monroe's claims and recommended that the same be referred to a select committee. In support of this motion it was argued that the Committee of Claims was overburdened with work; that the claim had last year been examined by a select committee, some of the members of which were still in the House; that complicated cases had often been referred to select committees in the past; that the evidence collected by the Ingham committee was not as complete as some members supposed; that the claims of Monroe against the government could not be fully and completely viewed except by a committee authorized to investigate and express an opinion on his dubious relations with Colonel Lane. In opposition to the motion it was said that the Committee of Claims was blind as justice, impartial, indefatigable, and known, not only to the House but to the nation, for its great labor and high intelligence; that a select committee was always pervaded by a strong infusion of friendly feeling towards the persons whose petitions it might be considering; that every claim should take the ordinary course. Why, asked one member, very possibly under the influence of the bottle, should an individual, because he lately has been the President of the United States, be awarded a courtesy which the House refused to the poor soldier who had fought its battles and who pleaded his wants or his wounds before it? [3]

The debate ended in a victory for the friends of Monroe. The Committee of Claims was discharged from the consideration of his case and it was referred to a select committee, again under the chairmanship of Representative Ingham. The opposition could console themselves with the thought that their arguments had not been rebutted but had been drowned out by the hisses and shouts of an abused and deluded public. For it was a fact that the utmost abhorrence had been expressed in the public streets, as well as elsewhere, at the great disrespect with which the ex-President had been treated by having his petition referred to the Committee of Claims.

The second Ingham committee reported on March 23, 1826.[4] Monroe had asked for $23,570 with interest from varying dates; the committee recommended that he be granted $15,533.53 with interest from December 3, 1810, the date of the last settlement of his accounts. The difference between the two sums they explained as follows: (1) They had disallowed his claim of $4,455 for interest on the outfit for his first mission partly because he had been told, at the time he was appointed, that no outfit would be allowed, and partly because, during a portion of the time for which interest was claimed, the government was somewhat in advance with him. (2) In the allowance of contingent expenses in his first mission to France and his mission to England, they had not adopted the highest sum given to other ministers but, in both cases, had taken the average sum paid to all American ministers at the respective governments as their guide in determining upon the allowance proper to be made to Monroe; by the application of this rule they had reduced Monroe's demand for his French mission from $3,515 to $1,495.85, and for his English mission from $2,000 to $437.68. The committee further explained that, in fixing December 3, 1810, as the period from which to commence the calculation of interest, they had been governed by the idea that interest ought not to run on a debt prior to its allowance by the accounting department; it must be assumed that delays in settlement were in some measure attributable to the claimants.

On May 12, a bill reported by the Ingham committee was debated. Monroe's friends eulogized his character and insisted on the value and importance of his many services; other members stated their objections to several items in the bill, but particularly to the allowance of interest. A vote having been taken on striking out this allowance, it passed in the affirmative, 90 to 73. The next day the bill was passed and sent to the Senate; it authorized and required the Secretary of the Treasury to pay Monroe the sum of $15,533.35.

If Monroe was disappointed by the refusal of the second Ingham committee to allow him interest on his outfit to France from 1803 to 1810 or to commence the calculation of interest on any of his admitted claims before December 3, 1810, his distress at being allowed no interest at all may easily be imagined. Fortunately the Senate proved more generous than the House. When the bill for Monroe's relief was brought to debate in that body, Senator Hugh L. White of Tennessee, chairman of the select committee to which the bill had been referred, moved to strike out the sum allowed by the House and to insert "$29,513,

THE CLAIMS OF 1825 AND THE ALLOWANCES OF 1826

Head of Account	Principal		Interest		Total	
	Claimed	Allowed	Claimed	Allowed	Claimed	Allowed
1. Additional salary—first mission	$ 2,750	$ 2,750	$ 4,721	$ 2,475	$ 7,471	$ 5,225
2. Additional contingent expenses—first mission	3,515	1,496	6,353	1,346	9,868	2,842
3. Interest on outfit—second mission	4,455	—	4,188	—	8,643	
4. Demurrage—second mission	350	350	478	315	828	665
5. Additional contingent expenses—second mission	2,000	437	2,425	394	4,425	831
6. Extraordinary expenses—second mission	10,500	10,500	12,101	9,450	22,601	19,950
Totals	$23,570	$15,533	$30,266	$13,980	$53,836	$29,513

in full of all demands against the United States." The additional $13,980 represented fifteen years' interest at 6 per cent on the principal sum granted by the House. After a lengthy discussion, during the course of which Senator William H. Harrison of Ohio, the future President, offered and withdrew a proposition to include interest on the outfit to France from 1803 to 1810, the amendment was accepted and the bill was passed. For a week the House resisted the Senate amendment, but on May 20, two days before adjourning, it receded from its disagreement. On the twenty-second the act was approved by President Adams.

VI

Further Claims and Allowances

In the ordinary operations of trade, when a creditor accepts a payment "in full of" all his demands against a debtor, he is precluded from urging upon the same debtor new or old claims founded upon transactions prior to the date of payment. But Monroe never felt himself bound by the prudent rules, or pusillanimous maxims, of commerce. While the second Ingham committee was considering his case, he had followed its proceedings from nearby Oak Hill, combatted through intermediaries [1] the too narrow principles upon which it proposed to make its report, and furnished it with memoranda, extracts of private letters, and other documents.

When the report was made, he had found himself in a difficult situation. It was possible that the whole amount of his claims might be obtained at another Congress, improbable at this. What should he do? Should he withdraw his claims now and bring them forward again in December

1827, when the Twentieth Congress would come together
for the first time? Or should he obtain a portion of them
immediately, ignore the proviso making the settlement final,
and rely on the indulgence of a future Congress to listen
to him without pleading a former recovery? Had he been
at ease, he would have had no difficulty in deciding this
question: he would rather have lost the whole than have
accepted less. But the interest of his family and creditors
must, from motives of honor, be considered; *his* pride
ought perhaps to give way to *their* necessities.[2] The action
of Congress in appropriating $29,513 in full of all of his
demands against the United States brought him to the
moment of decision. He accepted the money, assigned it to
the banks and individuals to whom it was due, and set
about obtaining more.

The task before him was not easy. He soon discovered
that the impression had got abroad that more had been
allowed him than was strictly due. At the same time he
found his conduct assailed in the public press in respect
of some occurrences with which he had been concerned
during the war of 1812. His first step must be to remove
the unfavorable impression and to vindicate his character
and conduct. Accordingly, during the summer of 1826,
he prepared a concise view of his claims and collected documents contradicting the misrepresentations to which he
had been subjected. In November, acting upon the advice
of John McLean, Postmaster General, he transmitted the
completed work to Gales and Seaton at Washington, who

on the fifteenth of the month began its publication in the
National Intelligencer.

*The Memoir of James Monroe, Esq., relating to his Un-
settled Claims upon the People and Government of the
United States* consisted of three parts. In the *Memoir*
proper he spoke with becoming self-esteem of his services
to the nation in the several capacities in which he had been
employed; stated briefly the differences between the claims
which he had presented for his two missions and the decision made in Congress upon them; explained his delay in
making application for redress as a proof of respect; and
suggested, as a fair object of inquiry, whether the mere
payment of the sums withheld from him, with interest on
them, was the only reparation that ought to be made to
him, whether some indemnity was not due him for the
great and heavy losses that he had sustained by the withholding of the money from him.

In the remarks that accompanied this *Memoir* he examined in detail the objections that had been raised against
his claims, without adverting to the spirit with which these
objections had been urged nor to the quarter from which
they had come; applauded himself for asking neither punitive damages [3] nor compound interest; noticed a transaction
connected with his first mission that had resulted in a contingent debt which he would probably have to pay; and
drew attention to some more recent occurrences, not with
a view to pecuniary indemnity, but with the object of leaving a true relation of facts to the important judgment of his

fellow citizens, and of posterity. The documents constitut-
ing the third part of the *Memoir* illustrated and supported
the views urged in the two preceding parts.

Monroe can hardly have expected his *Memoir* to produce an immediate result. He was well aware that in the
last Congress only about fifty persons had understood his
claim; the rest had played safe and inclined to the negative.[4]
The present Congress was made up of the same individuals;
it would sit only from December to the beginning of
March; there was little hope that it would reopen in its
second session a subject that it had finally concluded in its
first. But in December 1827 a new, perhaps a better Congress would be sitting. It would be well to seize time by the
forelock and, in making his case comprehensible, prepare
the ground for its justification.

The scheme was a good one, but, for the time being, it
met with misfortune. In a cause like Monroe's it is not
enough to inform ignorance; it is necessary to conciliate
favor. And circumstances unconnected with his claim were
gradually embroiling Monroe with the partisans of Andrew
Jackson, and with Jackson himself. In the summer of 1826,
Samuel L. Southard, Secretary of the Navy, in the social
confidence of a convivial party, had criticized Jackson's
military movements at New Orleans and commended Monroe's exertions in preparing and providing supplies for the
defense of that place; these remarks had been tale-borne to
the hero and had produced upon him an effect which John
Quincy Adams likened to that of a scarlet blanket upon a
tiger.[5] In the ensuing controversy the friends of Jackson

vented their wrath upon Monroe himself, charging him, in effect, with neglect of duty in failing to put within reach of Jackson at New Orleans the implements of war.

Shortly afterwards, Monroe found himself caught up in a dispute between Crawford and Calhoun about his attitude as President toward Jackson's insubordination during the Seminole campaign of 1818. Jackson had always maintained that Monroe, through an unofficial agent, had distinctly authorized or encouraged him to disobey or deviate from the orders communicated to him from the War Department; for a time he had kept the letter of that agent, a parasite of his own called Johnny Rhea, as a voucher; but he had later destroyed it upon the request, so he thought, of Monroe himself. Now, in the heat of the presidential campaign, he was shown a letter of 1818, purloined from Calhoun, in which Monroe expressed disapproval of his actions. It smelled so much of deception, he himself tells us, that his hair stood on end for one hour. Nor did his fury abate when Monroe found it necessary to deny that he had ever violated his oath of office by giving his sanction, privately or publicly, to Jackson's unlawful acts.

To make matters worse, the Virginia supporters of Adams, meeting in convention at Richmond, early in 1828, nominated Monroe to a place on their electoral ticket. The unwelcome compliment might confirm the long-held suspicion of Jackson's friends that Monroe was hostile to the General's election.[6]

Monroe did what he could to placate his implacable adversary. He announced his neutrality in the coming elec-

tion to the Jackson committee of Aldie in Loudoun County,
Virginia, and he declined his own nomination as an Elec-
tor. He vindicated his conduct in relation to Jackson in
1814 and 1818 in a series of letters to Hugh L. White of
Tennessee, known to be one of the General's friends, and
to "Black Horse Harry" Lee, his principal ghost-writer.
He pleaded with, and secured the consent of, Southard not
to bring his name into the controversy between himself
and Jackson. And he suspended or abandoned the idea of
himself publishing a book against Jackson to go with his
book against Washington and his letter against Jefferson.[7]

But these efforts availed him little, and in the meantime
unforeseen events were damaging his case in Congress. In
a debate of February 1827 on the general appropriation
bill, attention was drawn to an act of May 1, 1810, fixing
the compensation of public ministers.[8] This act had continued the authority of the President to allow a minister
plenipotentiary up to $9,000 a year as compensation for all
his personal services and expenses, together with an outfit
of not more than one year's full salary, but it had limited
the occasion upon which an outfit might be granted to the
time of the minister's leaving the United States. Its purpose was twofold: to prevent the President from granting
a minister the whole expenses of his mission in lieu of outfit, and to confine to a single outfit the amount of money,
beyond the ordinary salary, that might be granted to a
minister for any one trip abroad. Had it been carried into
execution, its effect would have been to make necessary an
application to Congress itself for the grant of any sum,

compensatory of extraordinary expense, in excess of $9,000. But the law was opposed by the Executive; and it was easily eluded. A minister could be sent out for, say, two years, paid $27,000 in salary and outfit, recalled to America, and sent out again to another post with another salary and another outfit. Elusion, however, had been unnecessary; for the Secretary of State had presently placed upon the law such a construction as to permit the allowance of an outfit not only to a minister leaving the United States but to one moving from one foreign court to another. This construction, founded, so it was said, on custom and usage, had left the law dead upon the statute books.

Mention of this act could hardly fail to be embarrassing to Monroe; for the settlement of the accounts of his second mission had been made while the act was on its passage through Congress. Had that settlement been governed by the terms of the act, he could have been allowed by the Executive Department only $9,000 as an outfit for the whole term of his stay abroad. As it was, he was allowed more than $29,700—an outfit to France, an outfit to England, and the whole of his expenses to Spain. A claim for $8,000 or $9,000 more, under the heads of interest on the outfit withheld from 1803 until 1810, and interest on that interest from 1810 until paid, might have invited the attention of Congress to a comparison better left unnoticed. Nor could it have helped Monroe to be named as the Secretary of State who, in construing the act of 1810, had effectively repealed it.

Another incident, occurring during the same debate,

proved equally embarrassing. Ingham, holding in his hand
the documents furnished by Monroe in 1825 to justify
(1) his receipt of a sum exceeding three outfits for his second mission and (2) his claim to more than a fourth outfit
for his detention in England, attacked the allowances reported therein to have been made to Adams and Clay for
their mission to Ghent. Inasmuch as Ingham, during the
last session, had used these same documents to obtain a
judgment of Congress in favor of Monroe, he seemed now
to be impeaching his own witnesses, discrediting his own
papers. In respect of the allowance to Adams, it was soon
discovered that the record was in error; but this finding
could only suggest that Monroe's case was not as well
vouched as it had once seemed to be. Nor was that case
strengthened when it was brought to light that the allowances complained of had been finally made to Adams and
Clay by Monroe himself while President. It might too easily be alleged that Monroe, in pointing to precedents of his
own manufacture, had imposed on the credulity, rather
than relied on the justice, of Congress.

These incidents happened in 1827. While the election of
1828 was in progress, Monroe could do little to focus the
attention of Congress or of the public upon his ancient
injuries. Early in that year, however, he permitted or persuaded his friends in Albemarle to republish the *Memoir*
which in 1826 he had put in the columns of the *National
Intelligencer*. A certain number of copies were reserved for
his use, and he placed them where they would do the most
good. Some he sent to powerful friends; others to the gov-

ernors of the several states for preservation in the executive archives; still others, perhaps, to colleges. We may suppose, too, that, acting on the advice of the Postmaster General, he sent a batch to Washington. McLean, in offering to converse occasionally with the influential members of Congress on the subject of his claim, had suggested that it could do no harm, and might be productive of some good, for them to read his *Memoir*.[9]

That Monroe hoped his claim would be taken up in the second session of the Twentieth Congress, beginning December 1, 1828, can hardly be doubted. But he proceeded with much circumspection. In encouraging this hope, McLean in August had given him a friendly warning: "You cannot move in this thing yourself, but your friends must do so."[10] And Monroe had replied: "P.S. with respect to my claims, the sentiment which you express in regard to them, has my entire concurrence. My land and slaves have all been sold in Albemarle: as has the tract of 20,000 acres in Clay County, Kentucky: in satisfaction of debts contracted in the public service, and large balances are still due. But I have no thought of taking any step, which might degrade the character of my country arising from the trusts with which I have been honoured, or be inconsistent with the well-vouched incidents of my past life."[11]

His first step was to send copies of his *Memoir* to his friends at Richmond to be presented to the members of the Virginia legislature. But, with anxious solicitude, he begged those friends to make it clear that he was not inviting a legislative interference in support of his claims. He wished

merely, out of respect for Virginia, to make the instances
of his public life and conduct more generally known to
his fellow citizens.[12]

His second step was to countenance, by silence or by dis-
creet inquiries, the efforts of his friends to obtain signa-
tures to a memorial of the citizens of Albemarle praying
Congress to reconsider his claims and to remunerate him
for his losses and sacrifices in the public service.

Unequal success attended his efforts. The Virginia As-
sembly was pervaded by impressions unfavorable to Monroe and, with unfeeling correctness, it did nothing where
nothing was asked. The citizens of Albemarle, however,
sent their memorial to Congress where on January 28, 1829,
it was referred in the House of Representatives to a select
committee.

This memorial was an important document, for it introduced Congress to a new set of claims based upon a new
principle.[13] Hitherto Monroe had founded his claims on
positive injuries allegedly sustained from the government
itself by the refusal of justice, by the strict standard of
right, in matters of account for services rendered. The
memorialists of Albemarle now suggested that he had other
claims which, though not precisely of this description,
were based on the immutable principles of justice and sanctioned by the surest policy which can govern a free state.

Monroe, they pointed out with angry sorrow, had been
fifty years in the service of his country. He had begun as
a young man of ample property; now, in the retirement
of his old age, he was suffering from the grievous calami-

ties of poverty. Was it not obvious that if, instead of sacrificing himself on the altar of his country, he had applied those fifty years, the prime of his life, to his own private affairs, to the improvement of his property and the enlargement of his pecuniary resources, a very different result would have followed from his exertions? Was it right, was it just, that a citizen who had devoted his life to his country in its highest stations, with integrity and fidelity, should be ruined by his services and his family deprived of the property which would otherwise have descended to them? Could a just, not to say a generous, nation, behold unmoved this faithful servant embarrassed, distressed, overwhelmed, and finally, perhaps, imprisoned for debts contracted in her service, and not vindicate her own honor by his relief?

Descending from rhetoric to detail, the memorialists proposed a course of action. Monroe's sacrifices were of two kinds: those which had been forced upon him by the denial of justice in the settlement of his accounts and those which had resulted from his self-immolation on his country's altar. Congress had already remunerated him in part for his losses of the first class; let it now complete the work and grant him the balance of his previous claims. Losses of the second class were not susceptible of being stated in an account or supported by vouchers, but there were some services, beyond the call of duty, which Monroe had performed in his various public capacities, and for which he had never claimed nor received compensation. These, by way of an equivalent, could be formed into an account. As Secretary of War, Monroe had himself negotiated, or been responsible for the negotiation of, some $6,000,000 in loans by banks and corporations to the government. Had he been a private individual, he would have been allowed a premium of ½ or even 1 per cent for his agency;[14] let him now be allowed the proper commission with interest from 1814. As President, Monroe had thrice inspected the fortifications of the country. Had he been a military officer, his expenses, say $10,000, would have been borne by the government; let them be allowed now, with interest from 1817, 1818, or 1819, as the case might be.

The committee to which the Albemarle memorial was referred was selected according to custom from amongst the members friendly to its object;[15] its chairman was William C. Rives of Albemarle County, Virginia. On February 12, 1829, it made its first report.[16] Monroe, it contended, had not been fairly treated in 1826. He should have been allowed the full amount of his claims for the contingent expenses of his first mission to France and his mission to England; he should have been allowed interest, at 6 per cent, on the outfit for his second mission to France from 1803 until 1810 and interest on that interest from 1810 until paid; and in respect of every principal sum admitted, he should have been allowed interest, not merely from December 1810, but from the several periods when those sums accrued. Computing the amounts still due him, the committee arrived at a principal debt of about $7,500, and at a debt for interest amounting to nearly $17,000. In respect of the claims previously presented to the consideration of Congress, the total sum now due was $24,377.04.[17]

Next, the committee proposed to allow a claim never made by Monroe but at which he had begun to hint in his memoir of 1826. This was a claim for $10,000 as reimbursement for a loss suffered in a private transaction connected with his first mission to France.

The grounds upon which this claim rested were peculiar; and as they were very partially stated by the committee and by Monroe himself, it will be necessary to examine them with some care. What had happened was this. In 1795, Monroe had bought a house and pleasure ground in a retired part of Paris, to wit, at the foot of Montmartre, for the accommodation of himself and his family, intending to keep it until he set out for home. This was the famous Folie La Bouexière, built about 1750 for the Bacchic and venereal pleasures of a bachelor farmer-general. It lay between the Rue de Clichy and the Rue Blanche and consisted of a pavilion, constructed on the plans of Antoine-Michel Carpentier, the great French architect, and a garden designed by Chevaulet. The pavilion represented a temple consecrated to Apollo and the Muses, and all the allegories that entered into its composition and decoration were related to that idea.[18] An anecdote of the house, involving M. de la Bouexière, the celebrated Mlle. Deschamps, and another couple, may be found by the curious reader in the Paris police reports.[19] Boccaccio might have called it *The Tax-Farmer's Revenge;* unfortunately, it is too scabrous for reproduction on these pages.

For the Folie La Bouexière, Monroe and his wife had paid 73,500 livres.[20] The price was low, and Monroe was

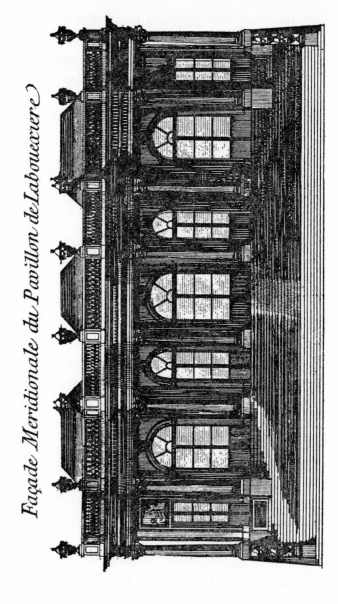

Façade Meridionale du Pavillon de Labouexere)

Façade Septentrionale

10 Toises

.1 2 3 4 5

envied by his friends. "I had heard," wrote Elbridge Gerry, "of your having made a fortunate purchase of a house to reside in which would appreciate in its value to a capital fortune. . . . I wish to receive from you an historical account of this extraordinary manoeuvre." [21] Monroe's removal, however, had disappointed these expectations. In 1797 he and his wife had sold the property for 100,000 livres, say $20,000, a sum that yielded them a profit, beyond the expense of repair, barely sufficient to defray their expenses in France and Holland during the last five months of their stay abroad.[22] In settlement with the purchaser, however, Monroe had not obtained all cash; because of some defect alleged in the title to the property, he had been paid in cash only half the amount stipulated; the other half he had borrowed from a fellow citizen, a friend, giving him a power to receive the balance when paid, if ever, with a mortgage on a tract of land in Clay County, Kentucky, of 20,000 acres, and a power to sell it, if necessary, whenever the necessity should arise. For thirty years the event was doubtful, but at last the French courts decided against the interests of Monroe. The purchaser was evicted from the property; and all hope of obtaining the unpaid half of the purchase money was lost. In 1827 the Kentucky acres were sold under the mortgage which Monroe had so confidently given.

In ordinary circumstances such a transaction, though it might have furnished matter for private and public condolences, could hardly have been made the foundation of a claim against the United States. But the circumstances were not ordinary. While Monroe had been in France, his purchase of a house had been turned against him. Rumors were circulated that he was deep in speculation, that he was buying up, at two years' purchase, the confiscated estates of the murdered or exiled friends of America. "It has even been propagated," he was informed by Madison, "that you and Skipwith, or perhaps you, through Skipwith, had purchased Chantilly, the magnificent estate of the late Prince of Condé." [23]

To these accusations Monroe upon his return home entered an indignant denial. All he had bought was his own residence—not Chantilly nor any other part of the national domain, but the private estate of M. Foulon, an architect who had remained his neighbor. He had, it was true, made a modest profit on the sale of the house, but even that profit had been in a measure accidental. At the time he purchased the house he had intended, when his mission was over, to offer it to the United States at the price he had given for it. He had been diverted from this design only by the manner of his recall and by the unhappy change which had taken place in Franco-American relations.[24]

Looking back at these facts and allegations in 1829, the Rives committee came to a generous conclusion. It might easily have suggested that inasmuch as Monroe had not been authorized to make the purchase, the government could be under no obligation to make good his loss. It might have added that had he in fact purchased for the United States, he would have been prohibited from selling without permission, and that, consequently, whatever obligation was imposed on the government by the purchase was released by the sale. It might have wondered how Monroe could ever have expected the United States to buy as an embassy a house with only six master rooms, even if the house itself might correctly be described as an immense palace.[25] But the committee was in no mood to quibble. It announced that Monroe had sacrificed his property in the public service and recommended that the amount of his loss, $10,000, should be included in the amount proposed to be paid to him.

Another claim never before asserted next engaged the attention or the emotions of the committee. In 1794, Monroe had obtained the release from prison of Thomas Paine, taken him into his house, supplied him for a year and a half with every necessary, and furnished him also with money, of which about 250 louis d'or were never repaid.

Monroe, in explaining his claims, had often mentioned this debt. He had even hinted that if justice were done him, the government would have repaid his advances to Paine as they had repaid his advances to Mme. de La Fayette. But he had never stated them in an account. On the contrary, he had taken great credit for his forbearance. "For my advances to Thomas Paine," he told the Ingham committee in 1825, "no claim was ever presented on my part, nor is any indemnity now desired."

It is not, however, to modesty that the historian will attribute Monroe's failure to charge this private debt to the government. Such a claim, had he presented it to the accounting officers of the Treasury, could not have been

allowed. Had he presented it to Congress, upon his return
from France, it would have been rejected. What Monroe
failed to point out was that his advances to Paine did not
stand upon the same ground as his advances to Mme. de
La Fayette. The latter had been made in pursuance of an
appropriation of $6,000 made by Congress for the relief
of La Fayette's family; they could lawfully be charged in
his public accounts. The former had been made by Monroe, out of the goodness of his heart, at his private risk.
What the accounting officers must have rejected might, to
be sure, have been allowed by Congress as a claim in
equity. But in the last years of the Federalist regime such
an allowance would surely have been denied. It was known
or supposed that Monroe's house was the rendezvous of all
Americans hostile to the Administration in Paris, and that
he himself had taken the lead in vilifying the President and
his Cabinet. Nor had Monroe been able to conceal the fact
that Thomas Paine, an inmate of his house and protected
by him, was writing against Washington and trying to influence the French government against the United States.
Representative Robert Goodloe Harper, indeed, as early
as 1797 had obtained a certificate to this effect, and notified
W. B. Giles, not yet estranged from Monroe, that he would
name the signer of the certificate if Monroe should deny
the fact.[26]

But in 1829 the circumstances surrounding Paine's debt
to Monroe were forgotten, and the Rives committee recommended that the government pay to Monroe the principal sum of 250 louis d'or, or $1,188, plus $2,423.52 as in-

terest thereon from April 1795. The grand total due him on his diplomatic account was $37,988.56.

Having admitted the whole of Monroe's previous claims and obtruded two new items into his account, the committee passed to a larger question: Ought Monroe to have been compensated, beyond his salary, for his services as Secretary of War and as President? In particular, should he now be allowed a reward for his agency in procuring loans to the government in 1814, or reimbursed for the expenses of his inspection tours during the three first summers of his presidential term?

In regard to the second part of this question, the committee declared itself unaware of any principle on which the reimbursement of those expenses could be assumed without forming a precedent of dangerous latitude. In regard to the first part, it reserved its views for a supplemental report.[27] Two weeks later it recommended that Monroe be paid $25,000 in consideration for his agency in procuring loans for the use of the government during the war of 1812.

To understand this last recommendation, it will again be necessary to look behind the committee's report to the facts.

In the autumn of 1814 the affairs of the nation were in a difficult conjuncture. Its capital city had been seized and its public buildings destroyed. Its inland and maritime frontiers, from the Great Lakes to the Penobscot and along the whole Atlantic coast, were invaded or menaced with invasion. Large forces had been called into action at every point. At the same time the Treasury was suffering under every kind of embarrassment. The demands upon it were great, and the means to satisfy them were small. Taxes were unproductive, for they were paid for the most part in evidences of debt. Bank credit had been rendered, in a great degree, useless by the stoppage of payments in specie and the consequent impracticability of transferring the public funds from their places of deposit, mainly in the South and West, to the places where they were needed to meet the public engagements. For the rest, the means available to the Treasury consisted, in the words of Secretary Alexander J. Dallas, "of the fragment of an authority to borrow, when nobody was disposed to lend, and to issue Treasury notes, which none but necessitous creditors, or contractors in distress, or commissaries, quartermasters, and navy agents, acting as it were officially, seemed willing to accept."

At this period the War Department was under the management of Monroe, but the Treasury Department was, for an interval of about a fortnight, without an effective head. George W. Campbell, Secretary of the Treasury, had resigned his office on September 26; his successor, Dallas, did not reach Washington until October 13; the acting Secretary, Samuel H. Smith, commissioner of the revenue, either could not or would not take a responsibility. Confronted by necessity, Monroe bestirred himself. Acting without authority of law, but with the sanction of the President, he negotiated contracts for loans, to the amount of about $5,000,000, from banks and corporations in Albany, New York, Philadelphia, Baltimore, Norfolk, Charleston, and elsewhere, which were later recognized by the Treasury Department. In addition, he borrowed upwards of a million dollars from banks in the District of Columbia simply, we are told by his clerk, by pledging the faith of the government to pay them, with legal interest, so soon as the Treasury was in a situation to furnish the funds.[28] Very possibly, in respect of this last million, the promises and, indeed, tears of the Secretary were reinforced by a more persuasive argument. In November 1814 it was stated in Congress that "the Government was subsisting upon the drainings of unchartered banks in the District, who felt themselves compelled to contribute their means, lest the rod, in terrorem, which was held over them, should be applied, and an act of incorporation refused." [29]

Such were the extra services rendered by Monroe while in the War Department. That fifteen years later they should have become the basis of a claim against the United States may furnish occasion for surprise; for in 1825 Monroe had invited the attention of the Ingham committee to these same services with the comment that for them he had "never asked, expected, or would receive, one cent." By 1829, however, he had changed his tune. He permitted the citizens of Albemarle to make the claim on his behalf. A year later he would notify Congress that he considered it *his duty* to present it.

In support of doubtful or extraordinary claims it is always useful to produce a precedent. The Rives committee had no difficulty in finding one in the allowances made in

1823 to "another distinguished patriot," Daniel D. Tompkins. With great wisdom, however, they refrained from examining this precedent in detail; nor did they think it pertinent to remark that its application to Monroe's case was the consequence of a decision made by Monroe himself upon a liberal, or a mistaken, construction of law.

During the War of 1812, Tompkins had occupied an anomalous position. He was Governor of New York, but at the same time he had acted as a sort of paymaster general for all the military forces within the state. In the latter capacity, as an agent of the federal government, he had disbursed the enormous sum of $1,982,000, for which he was held personally responsible and required to account at various bureaus of the Treasury and War Departments. The greater part of this sum, moreover, had been raised by his own exertions. Not only had he advanced his own funds to the government but also he had borrowed on his personal credit nearly $1,400,000 from various individuals and corporations, including the corporation of the city of New York. In taking upon himself the legal responsibility for repaying these loans, Tompkins was well aware that he was risking his fortune, but, urged on by the venerable Rufus King, he had yielded to the earnest entreaties of Madison and Monroe, coupled with their assurances that within thirty or forty days Treasury notes would be sent him to take up his obligations and, in effect, transfer the debt from the ostensible to the real borrower. In the event, Tompkins had been ruined. A part only of the promised notes were sent in proper time to relieve him; the city corporation pressed him for repayment; and he was held up to the public as a defaulter. Furthermore, upon the settlement of the accounts of his disbursing agency, he was charged with all the losses incurred by the frauds and failures of the subagents to whom money had been advanced through his hands.

In due course, that is to say about nine years later, Congress decided to indemnify him. Accordingly it passed a law authorizing the accounting officers of the Treasury to adjust and settle the accounts of Daniel D. Tompkins on principles of equity and justice, subject to the revision and final decision of the President of the United States. It was in executing this law that Monroe, as President, produced the precedent which the Rives committee later noticed as applicable to his own case.

A law directing the settlement of an account upon principles of equity and justice related, at this period of history, to the degree of evidence receivable at the Treasury and not to the claims or items composing the account. A claimant, for example, if he could not adduce a voucher, might resort to his oath; but he was not permitted to make any unusual, extraordinary, or unlawful demand upon the government. In the case of Tompkins, however, it was clear that Congress intended something more. Monroe accordingly turned to the report of the committee raised upon Tompkins' accounts to ascertain the true extent and meaning of the law. There, among other things, he found a recommendation that it would be just and reasonable to allow a reasonable commission to Tompkins on all moneys

disbursed by him during the war. In pursuance of this recommendation, Monroe allowed him a commission of 5 per
cent on these disbursements. In reporting his action to
Congress, he explained it as follows: "I have made him this
extra allowance in consideration of the aid which he afforded to the Government at that important epoch in obtaining the loan of a considerable part of the sum thus disbursed."

It was in this explanation that the idea was introduced
for the first time that a commission might be allowed on
the receipts as well as on the disbursements of a salaried
officer. Monroe had manufactured a precedent which, with
some stretching, might be made to cover his own case. It
would only be necessary to gloss over the difference between a man who raises money on his own responsibility
and who disburses it at personal risk and a man who raises
money on the responsibility of others and who disburses it
at the risk of the Treasury.

Yet the Rives committee, although they pointed to Monroe's allowance to Tompkins in justifying their own allowance to Monroe, were unwilling to be bound by the logic
of analogy. Rejecting the idea that they were either setting or following a precedent, they declared that Monroe's
case was unique, "*sui generis*, without similitude in this
our day, nor never can be. No second war of the Revolution will be recorded on the pages of our history; and
nearly all the heroes of that memorable day are out of the
reach of this precedent, and of every other human regula-
tion; and not one of the few survivors . . . has, like this

last of the Mohicans, such strong claims on the gratitude and best feelings of this nation." This rhetoric might not have been entirely pleasing to Monroe, for it seemed to suggest that his claim was to favor and indulgence rather than to right and justice.

However this may be, the two reports of the Rives committee were not unfavorable to Monroe. In sum they recommended that he be paid upwards of $60,000, two wagon loads of Spanish milled dollars, in the words of an unfriendly Congressman, in addition to the $29,513 which he had collected in 1826.

When these reports were received, the Twentieth Congress was on the verge of adjournment. In the few remaining days of the session no attempt was made to consider them. Monroe's business therefore lay dormant for a year. The Twenty-first Congress, elected with Jackson in 1828, met for the first time in December 1829. Two months later, at the instance of Charles F. Mercer of Loudoun County, Virginia, an anti-Jackson friend of Monroe's, another select committee [30] of the House of Representatives was raised on the Albemarle memorial. After deliberating for three weeks it reported a bill to direct the Secretary of the Treasury to pay Monroe the sum of $67,980.96.[31]

The items composing this aggregate were the same as those reported by the Rives committee with two exceptions. The members of the Mercer committee retrenched the allowance of interest upon interest on the outfit of Monroe's second mission to France—a saving to the public of $4,423.95. But at the same time they increased the commission to be paid for his agency in procuring loans in 1814 from $25,000 to $37,028.93. Instead of allowing him a flat sum, fixed more or less arbitrarily, on the whole of his borrowings, they proposed to give him a commission of 2½ per cent on that portion of those borrowings that was raised in the District of Columbia.

In justifying this mode of calculation they suggested that the whole of these moneys had not only been raised but had also been disbursed by Monroe, an allegation which might give the transaction the appearance of a large disbursing agency on Monroe's part. In this manner they improved the analogy between Monroe's case and that of Governor Tompkins and were able to mention the precedent of Commodore Isaac Chauncey, who had borrowed no money but who had been allowed by Congress a commission on the millions which had passed through his hands to finance the war that "raged among the ship carpenters at Sackett's Harbor and Kingston for the supremacy of Lake Ontario." [32]

The report of the Mercer Committee was received by the House on March 6, 1830; but again there was delay. Congress adjourned at the end of May without taking any action on it. Still the outlook was hopeful. Congress was in a generous mood. By a decided majority it had established a construction of the Revolutionary pension laws more liberal than that which they had received from the Secretary of War; as a Revolution man, Monroe might expect to be treated with the same openhearted spirit. Nor did it pass unnoticed that President Jackson in a document

annexed to his veto of the Maysville Road bill, had listed
Monroe's claim as a charge upon the Treasury even though
the bill for paying it had been passed by neither House.[33]

Monroe in the meantime had not been idle. While the
committees of the House were considering his claims, he
propitiated favor and disarmed severity. Rives, who had
formerly been not very zealous in his interest, was brought
round by his kindness.[34] William F. Gordon, who replaced
Rives and who had formerly associated with Monroe's
enemies, became the object of the ex-President's solicitude.
Southard was persuaded to bear in silence the attacks of
Jackson as long as Monroe's claim might be undecided.
Calhoun was urged not to bring his dispute with Jackson
before the public. In November 1829, Monroe had even
dined with Jackson. The two Presidents sat side by side
and were observed in earnest conversation; whether they
touched upon the subject of Monroe's claims cannot be
stated, for they were not overheard; but it was noticed that
there was a great appearance of cordiality between them
and that Jackson affected to treat Monroe with affectionate
respect and kindness. At this same dinner Tench Ringgold,
Monroe's devoted friend, sat between John H. Eaton, the
Secretary of War, and W. C. Lewis of the Kitchen Cabinet; Ringgold seized the opportunity to tell them that
Monroe had always been the ardent friend of General Jackson and particularly had supported him against the opinions
of his Cabinet in the affair of the Seminole War.[35] But
Monroe was careful not to antagonize the New England
interest. In December 1830 he spoke at length with John

Quincy Adams about his difficulties with Jackson and complained that Jackson had treated him very ill.[36]

Having paved the way for a new démarche, Monroe on November 20, 1830, addressed a letter to the Speaker of the House of Representatives demanding action on the bill for his relief.[37] In this communication he explained once more the ancient injuries for which he had received so pitiful a compensation; justified the new items of account which had been brought forward in his behalf and for which he now accepted responsibility; and illustrated the whole with a retrospect of the interesting occurrences to which he had been a party since 1794.

One incident that he related seemed of a character to form the basis of a new claim. On his second mission to Europe he had performed an extra service. Fearful that Bonaparte would refuse to execute the treaty ceding Louisiana to the United States, he had paid him a portion of the stipulated purchase money in advance of the ratification of the treaty by the American government. Liberally construing the power under his instructions over the $2,000,000 voted by Congress for the purchase of Florida, he had guaranteed to the two great houses of Hope and Baring ten million francs, which they then paid to Talleyrand. In so doing, he had incurred a great risk. Had anything occurred to prevent the execution of the treaty, he would have been deeply censured, perhaps ruined. But his daring had been successful. He had bound the First Consul by the irresistible tie of personal honor, and the United States had gained the benefit. Monroe, it is true, made no claim for a commission on this extraordinary disbursement; he had mentioned it only as an instance of his conduct in affairs involving a great responsibility for money. But those who recollected the history of other such recitations might have been pardoned for thinking that the disclosure of this hitherto secret service might be preliminary to a discovery by Monroe of his duty to present a claim for it.

However this might be, Monroe's letter was read in the House of Representatives on December 13 and referred to the Committee of the Whole, already charged with the bill for his relief. Presently it was reinforced by another paper signed by the citizens of Albemarle and by a memorial from his new neighbors, the citizens of the City of New York.[38] The paper from Albemarle instructed Representative William F. Gordon to press Congress for action. The New York memorial was an appeal to Congress to treat with liberality a man who had, by the splendor of his actions and the purity of his life, contributed to elevate his country in the scale of nations. Its flavor may be tasted in an extract. "Look upon a man once 'the observed of all observers' occupying a station that might attract the envy of a world: now broken in health and enfeebled by age— prevented by embarrassments from dispensing the hospitalities of his paternal mansion—debarred almost from the hope that his eyes may be closed on the soil of his birth." Walter Bowne, Mayor of New York, presided over the meeting that got up the memorial; Philip Hone was one of the vice presidents. Yet it was intimated in Congress that the memorialists were Monroe's creditors rather than his friends.

The proceedings which followed were not well calculated to sooth the sensibilities, or nourish the pride, of the impoverished President. In Committee of the Whole House on the State of the Union, "that dead sea of the House" as Representative Peyton was later to call it, a root-and-branch attack was launched against the bill. Amongst others, Lewis Williams of North Carolina, the most experienced member of the House in matters of claims and accounts, expressed his conviction that Monroe's claim was wholly destitute of foundation. In the United States (he began) all men are equal; separate or exclusive privileges and immunities were not to be allowed to anyone. If a law be passed for the benefit of any one individual, its principle must be made applicable to every other citizen similarly situated. And what was the ground of Monroe's claim? Simply that the compensation allowed by law had proved inadequate to his expenses. But everyone who takes an office is presumed to know the salary attached to it. When he enters upon the discharge of his duty, it must be supposed that he is satisfied with it; let him then be content with his salary and regulate his expenditures accordingly. Admit the opposite principle, pass this bill, and what will be the consequence? In effect, Congress will have proclaimed to the world that every officer is at liberty to expend just as much as he pleases; that his habits of waste and extravagance, if he has any, need not be corrected; that if, by improvidence in his past life, he should become indigent or embarrassed in his old age, government will sustain and support him. Such must be the calculation of everyone who takes an office, and has a disposition to expend more money than the salary allowed by law.

In response to this general attack, which Williams and others supported by a particular examination of each separate item in his account, the friends of Monroe resorted, perhaps could resort, only to the language of eulogy. They told of his early, constant, and devoted patriotism; of his long, arduous and valuable services; of his sufferings, of his wants, and distresses. And they suggested that the eyes of the world were upon America; that the appropriation should be made to avoid the reproaches which would be cast from abroad upon a government willing to permit James Monroe to expire in poverty. These remonstrances, however, were addressed to deaf ears and unfeeling hearts. Elisha Whittlesey of Ohio, chairman of the Committee of Claims, who was later to win fame in the accounting profession as Comptroller of the Treasury, moved to destroy the bill by striking out its enacting clause. The committee supported him by a vote of 78 to 67; then it rose and reported the truncated remains of the bill to the House.

Yet all was not lost. Monroe himself was his own best advocate. While claiming nothing but what should appear strictly due to him on sound principles, on full consideration and on unquestionable evidence, he lost no opportunity of emphasizing the magnitude of his debts and the difficulties of his present situation. The very accidents of his life supported his claims to justice with an appeal to sympathy. His health infirm, his appearance feeble and emaciated, afflicted by the recent loss of his wife and a favorite son-in-law, he was residing far from his native country, in New York, a pensioner of the postmaster of that city, Samuel L. Gouverneur, another son-in-law. His supporters in Congress could say, with little fear of contradiction, that if the decision of his claim were submitted to the people of the nation, their decision would be almost unanimous in his favor.

But more active forces were at work in his behalf. Gouverneur was in Washington lobbying for his claim. John Sergeant, the famous Philadelphia lawyer, was writing to his friends and helping in every way.[39] Silas Burrows, who only recently had received the formal thanks of the government of the United States for a signal act of humanity and disinterested magnanimity, had gone to the seat of government for no other reason than to prevail upon Congress to pass the bill in Monroe's favor. Burrows had converted Rollin C. Mallary of Vermont and had engaged John Quincy Adams to work the conversion of John W. Taylor of New York. He had also dined privately with President Jackson and received public marks of esteem from Martin Van Buren, both of whom were eager to detach him from the Clay interest in the coming presidential election.[40] Letter writers at Washington were furnishing the editors of papers throughout the country with statements reflecting on the conduct of members of the House of Representatives, some for voting against, others for inattention to, the claim. These letters were published and the papers sent to Washington with the object, it is scarcely uncharitable to suppose, of influencing the final vote upon the question. The gentle art of persuasion, or the severer discipline of intimidation, was applied with particular solicitude to the minds and feelings of the members from Virginia, for it was with them that the great difficulty lay.

Defeated in Committee of the Whole, the friends of Monroe resumed the assault in the House. Presently it became clear that some accommodation would be made. Mercer proposed one compromise, Williams another. Finally, Joseph Hemphill, a Jackson Democrat from Pennsylvania, found the solution. Let Congress forget about the items in Monroe's account and simply appropriate a lump sum "for public services, losses, and sacrifices" to be paid to Monroe, immediately after the passing of the act, out of any money in the Treasury not otherwise appropriated, such payment to be "in full of all demands of the said James Monroe for his claims aforesaid."

This idea, after a brief debate, was adopted by a vote of 105 to 92, with an amendment offered by Abraham Rencher of North Carolina. The sum of $30,000 was fixed upon as proper to quiet Monroe, but it was provided that this amount should be paid him only if the accounting officer of the Treasury should, upon an examination of his accounts, believe so much was due him upon the principles of equity and justice.

The bill now went to the Senate, where it encountered further difficulties. Although a select committee [41] reported in its favor, and although, as early as February 16, the presiding officer of the Senate, Calhoun, told Monroe that it would probably pass, its place on the calendar was such that it could probably not be reached in the regular order before adjournment. The danger was averted by the energy of Senator John M. Clayton of Delaware, who persuaded Robert Y. Hayne of South Carolina to make a motion of a type to which he was in general opposed, namely to take the bill up out of turn. The motion prevailed; the bill was called up; an amendment reported by the committee to strike out the words "for public services, losses, and sacrifices," was defeated, on the motion of Hayne, to save time; then, by a division of 22 to 15, the bill was passed. In the evening of the same day, March 2, 1831, it was signed by President Jackson and became law.

The final settlement of Monroe's claims was greeted with a sigh of relief by such of his friends as were waiting to resume their quarrels with President Jackson. On March 31, Samuel Southard wrote to Monroe reminding him that he had tried to keep his name out of the controversy between himself and Jackson lest some of Jackson's friends in Congress be rendered adverse to his claims; but now the claim had passed and was before the Treasury; how was it progressing and when would it be closed? Calhoun was more impatient. At midnight, February 16, while Monroe's claim was still before the Senate, he published his pamphlet against Jackson and Crawford.

But Monroe himself was far from pleased at the turn of events. It did not escape his notice that of the Virginia delegation in the House fourteen members had voted against the bill and only five for it. More important, the sum voted him by Congress fell far short of his expectations and calculations. And the mode of granting it might seem insulting. He was to be paid $30,000 "for public services, losses, and sacrifices"; but a particular meaning had been given to these words by the Virginia Senators in a contemporaneous debate on another item of appropriation; a compensation for public services, unlike a compensation for outfit and expenses, was to be regarded as a donation founded on indulgence rather than as the payment of a lawful debt.[42]

Nor could Monroe fail to be reminded by the phrase of the sarcastic amendment offered to it in the House by a Jacksonian Democrat from North Carolina. Robert Potter, lumping together all the public moneys ever allowed to Monroe, including his salary as President, had suggested that after the word *sacrifices*, the following clause should come in: "in addition to the $400,000, heretofore paid to said James Monroe, for the same consideration." Furthermore, Monroe must have read with indignation the sentence which made this appropriation a payment "in full of all demands of the said James Monroe for all his claims aforesaid," for he could hardly fail to recollect the question asked by Lewis Williams in respect of it: "Would it be of any avail? The act formerly passed for the relief of James Monroe contained a similar provision, but it had not prevented the introduction of the present bill."

These were matters that touched his honor; but there was also a difficulty that touched his pocket. The act required him to satisfy the accounting officer of the Treasury of the justice and equity of his claim; and this, according to his own assertion, he flatly refused to do. "The accounting officers," he wrote to Madison on April 11, "have made no decision in my claims, and have given me much trouble. I have told them that I would make out no account adapted to the act, which fell far short of making me a just reparation, and that I had rather lose the whole sum than give to it any sanction, be the consequences what they may." [43]

These remarks might have puzzled the officers of the Treasury had they known of them. For when they had called upon Monroe for an account under the act for his relief, he had replied at length to his old friend Samuel D. Ingham, now Secretary of the Treasury, and submitted two accounts, one to the Fifth Auditor, Stephen Pleasonton, for diplomatic losses and sacrifices, the other to Peter Hagner, Third Auditor, for commissions on loans negotiated and disbursed in 1814.[44] These, it is true, had not been prepared for the occasion. They were adaptations of the statements got up two years earlier by Mr. Rives for the use of the committee of which he was chairman. They suggested that, as of March 1829, Monroe was entitled to $37,988.56 on diplomatic account and to $37,028.27 for commissions.

In rendering these accounts Monroe made it clear that he regarded the sums too small. The diplomatic account, for example, contained an item of $10,000 for the loss sustained in the sale of his house in Paris in 1797; but where was the interest for thirty-four years, another $20,400? The account for commissions showed only a single item—

2½ per cent on the capital sum of the loans negotiated in the District of Columbia; but where was the commission on the other millions that he had borrowed elsewhere? Monroe indicated also that, if the act for his relief had not restricted the sum that might be allowed him to a precise and limited amount, he would have invited the attention of the accounting officers to a number of other heavy sacrifices for which he deserved compensation; he had lost money on the sales of his tract above Charlottesville, of the rest of his property in Albemarle, and of his acres in Kentucky.

Nowhere did Monroe say that he would refuse to accept whatever might be allowed him. On the contrary, he suggested that the accounting officer fix the grant of $30,000 in whatever mode might appear to him most proper. Then he added: "In accepting it, although I shall make no further claim, let the consequences to me be what they may, I wish it to be understood, that it will fall far short of what [*words cut out*] to be justly due to me."

On April 7, Stephen Pleasonton transmitted to Comptroller Anderson for his decision a statement of Monroe's diplomatic account. By disallowing the claim nearest to Monroe's heart, the interest on his outfit to Paris from 1803 to 1810 and the interest on that interest from 1810 to date, by adding two years' interest on various items to bring the account up to 1831, and by making a few minor adjustments, Pleasonton fixed the sum due at $29,192.50.[45]

Anderson, however, rejected this report as not coming wholly within the meaning of the act. Pleasanton on April 12 then produced another report simply certifying that the sum of $30,000 was due to Monroe upon principles of justice and equity. The next day Anderson signified his concurrence: "According as I do—with the views and opinion of the 5th Auditor—as expressed in the within report —I do hereby admit and certify it accordingly." [46]

On April 13, Peter Hagner returned to Secretary Ingham the papers relative to Monroe's war loans. It was useless to settle them, for the appropriation to pay them was exhausted.

The long struggle was now over. On April 21, Madison congratulated Monroe that the sum voted to him had "escaped the loppings to which it was exposed from the accounting process at Washington" and that he was so far relieved from the vexations involved in it.[47] On April 27 John Quincy Adams visited Monroe in New York and learned that the allowance of $30,000 had been paid him.[48]

On May 16, in a codicil to his will, Monroe extended the trust of his son-in-law, Samuel L. Gouverneur, to whom he had committed the management of all his concerns, "to the grant lately made by Congress, which I have authorized him to enter and dispose of, in his own name, well knowing that he will apply it in that way, with more advantage than if entered in mine.[49] On May 28 he had the satisfaction of receiving a letter from Representative Dutee J. Pearce of Rhode Island, who informed him that the Eastern members who had voted for his claim were actuated by justice alone and thought the sum too small.[50] About a month later, on July 4, 1831, he died.

VII

The Reasons Why

To the candid reader the history of Monroe's claims must appear altogether extraordinary. It might seem to contradict Jefferson's early estimate of his honesty: "He is a man whose soul might be turned wrong side outwards without discovering a blemish to the world." [1] For certainly Monroe's course was devious in preferring these claims against the public. That he preferred them at all must occasion surprise.

Monroe's own explanation of his action is far from satisfactory: poverty had compelled him to assert his right. Had he been rich, or even moderately well off, nothing could have induced him to reopen these old accounts; but he was poor, and he owed a duty not only to himself but also to his family and his creditors. His ultimate distress had been due to a single cause: He had been unjustly treated by the Executive Department in the settlement of the accounts of his two missions to Europe. From both missions he had returned home charged with debts which, in their consequence, had borne heavily upon him through life. Had he been paid what he was due, when it was due, he might have been able to discharge those debts; perhaps he would never have had to incur them. Certainly he could have made some arrangement with his creditors that would have saved his lands or permitted him to choose a favorable season for their sale. Delicacy had silenced him for many years; but now necessity forced him to speak up.

Part of this explanation we may accept without cavil. We may concede that, in 1825 and afterwards, Monroe asked Congress for money because his affairs were so embarrassed that he could not go on without it. His poverty was undeniable. To his contemporaries it might even seem paradoxical; for the disappearance of Monroe's estate could not be explained by any sudden revolution in the Wheel of Fortune. His name could not be entered "in the rufull Register of mischief and mishap" as one of the many magistrates "whom unfriendly Fortune did trayne unto a trap." Quite the contrary. As John Quincy Adams put the matter in 1831: "Mr. Monroe is a very remarkable instance of a man whose life has been a continued series of the most extraordinary good fortune, who has never met with any known disaster, has gone through a splendid career of public service, has received more pecuniary reward from the public than any other man since the existence of the nation, and is now dying, at the age of seventy-two, in wretchedness and beggary." [2]

The historian, however, must reject Monroe's suggestion

that his ruin was occasioned by the injustice of the Executive Department. Such a suggestion could impose only on
those who were unfamiliar with the history of the settlement of his accounts, who had not examined his claims in
detail, or who had not tested them by the laws and usages
which regulated and controlled the admission of credits in
all analogous cases. Those who saw to the bottom of Monroe's pecuniary transactions with the government must
have acquitted the Executive of every imputation of injustice—unless, indeed, they chose to consider the generosity
with which he had been treated as a dereliction of duty to
the public.

The causes of Monroe's distress were quite different.
They may be traced to a variety of circumstances which
in combination must have ruined every man of modest
patrimony. In a new country the pecuniary rewards of
public office are seldom commensurate to the expenses that
they are intended to defray. A minister of the United States
at Paris or London could draw from the bankers under the
head of salary no more than $9,000 per year; yet the nor-
mal costs of his mission at these expensive posts could
scarcely be met at a lower rate of salary than $12,000 or
even $15,000 a year.[3] It was a proverb of the times that no
American minister could live in Europe without trenching
upon his own funds.[4] According to Edward Everett, the
cost of maintaining Dr. Franklin in republican simplicity
at the Court of France exceeded $14,000 a year, while
Chancellor Livingston, during his short residence at the
same court, in addition to his allowances from the govern-

ment, sank an estate of $100,000.[5] Nor could Monroe hope to recoup his losses from the salaries of a Secretary of State or President, for these, too, were inadequate to the charges that must fall upon them.

The niggardliness of Congress in respect of public salaries must equally affect every officer of government in a situation similar to Monroe's. But in his foreign posts Monroe suffered also from what may be called a sectional disadvantage. He was a Southerner; and it was often noticed that losses "were the inevitable accompaniment of every Southern man whose care is abstracted from his domestic concerns." [6] Monroe himself, or the Albemarle memorialists on his behalf, conceded that a portion of his lands had been "sacrificed by unavoidable neglect, arising from his employment in the public service in foreign countries, too far distant for him to extend any salutary control over these possessions." [7]

But some part of Monroe's troubles must be attributed to a defect in his own character. It is difficult to read the accounts of his style of living at Paris and London, in conjunction with the warnings given him by Jefferson against extravagance, without feeling that he was infected by a spirit of emulous ostentation, a desire to keep up with the richest men of the first fashion.

Lastly, we may notice the effect of accident upon his fortune—the necessity that he was under, whether induced by family pride or fraternal affection, to assume the heavy debts of his scapegrace brother.

These are the explanations of Monroe's pecuniary em-

barrassments that might satisfy the historian. They were
not, as we have seen, those advanced by Monroe himself.
Yet it is difficult to believe that Monroe really thought
himself entitled to blame the accounting officers of the
Treasury, the Secretary of State, or the President for not
allowing him credits that he never asked, credits that he
voluntarily relinquished, credits that he declared himself
unwilling to accept, or credits that were not within the
competence of any executive officer to admit. His own
assertion or boast that he had never, before 1825, pressed
his claims on any branch of the government cannot be
reconciled with the charge that he had suffered injustice
in their settlement.

Why then did he make the charge? The answer, may,
perhaps, be sought in his pride. He asked Congress for
money because he was poor, but he could not bring himself
to ask it as a gift or as a general reward to be granted out
of respect for great characters and public services. "I wish
it to be understood," he repeatedly told Congress, "that,
in regard to my claims, I ask no indulgence or favor; that
I ask nothing which is not strictly due me on sound principles, and which my country shall on full consideration
and unquestionable evidence, think that it owes it to itself
to allow me." [8] By pretending that his claims had some
foundation in law or equity, Monroe might, in his own
eyes, sustain his character and convince himself that he
was appealing to the justice of his country rather than to
its gratitude.

Poverty, moreover, was not the only motive that brought

Monroe to Congress. In the declining years of his life his embarrassments were not wholly pecuniary. In 1817 he had come into power almost by acclamation; and immediately he had found his popularity waning. His tour of observation through the North was attributed by his friends to a desire of soothing the spirit of party rancor; but by others it was traced to that vanity which is flattered by public pageantries—to a servile disposition to propitiate political enemies. From that moment, we are told,[9] an opposition sprang up to his Administration. Three of his "lieutenants took the field for the Empire, while he sat as an incubus on the Government." Each assailed the department of his rival and subjected its policies to the bitterest invective. The spirit of opposition being thus engendered, the President's administration was pronounced weak and prodigal; and, even upon the floor of the House of Representatives, he was charged with using public money for private purposes. As his second term drew to a close, it was one of John Randolph's common sayings that "Mr. Monroe came into power by universal consent, and he would go out with equal unanimity."[10]

Even after leaving office, Monroe heard his character attacked, his achievements denied or depreciated. The remarks of his ancient enemies he might bear with some composure. But he must have read with indignation the published opinions of the friends of his youth. John Randolph, in 1826, compared him to "that scoundrel, Aaron Burr, though not greater than him who formed the union of honest men of all parties."[11] Edward Livingston, although he supported in both House and Senate Monroe's demands for money, refused to allow him the whole credit for the acquisition of Louisiana.[12] William Branch Giles, while Governor of Virginia, wrote continually against him in the columns of the Richmond *Enquirer*, pronouncing him a failure in every office he had ever held and a man who, for the benefit of his own pocket, "had turned his old mantle of Republican true blue into a new one of artificial, despotic black!!! Not one of the old federal black, but a new one of the deepest, despotic dye!!!" Giles would not even commiserate with him in his distress. On the contrary, he proclaimed him a public pauper, whom the United States must, as they always had, continue to support; he was undeserving of sympathy; still less did he have a right to demand it: ". . . the last who ought to call out for pity and compassion are those who push themselves into public offices without the capacity to discharge the duties of them." [13]

Such strictures and cavils were well suited to irritate the sensibilities and arouse the anger of a man whose leading characteristic had always been the thirst of praise. If poverty first induced Monroe to ask Congress for money, the desire of vindicating his character and services might have suggested the particular items that should constitute his claims.

The great injuries suffered by Monroe at the hands of the Executive were, in fact, not pecuniary; nor had they anything to do with the settlement of his accounts. He had been dismissed from office in 1796 by a man whom in 1825 he no longer dared attack. At the same time he had been accused of speculating with public money, of feasting his friends at public expense, and of harboring in his house the enemies of public policy. He had been slighted in 1806 by the appointment of Pinkney as his coadjutor and insulted in 1807 by Jefferson's summary rejection of his British Treaty. He had found his claim disputed, that the acquisition of Louisiana was the consequence of his own great exertions and diplomatic skill. He had been criticized for charging to the public the court dress in which his wife had been presented to Bonaparte. He had been blamed for ostentatious living and reproached for returning from the glittering courts of Europe with a mind very different from that which he had carried there. His conduct during the War of 1812 had been impugned. He had been painted by General Armstrong as a military incompetent [14] and by Governor Giles as a simpleton easily parted from the public's money. As President, he had been charged with embezzling the funds specifically entrusted to his control, and it had even been suggested (by Governor Giles) that his conduct in respect of Spain was such as to justify his removal from office by the mode pointed out in the Constitution.

The claims that Monroe chose to prefer against the government of his country might individually be destitute of legal foundation; but taken in the aggregate, they afforded him the oportunity to review and defend his whole life as a servant of the United States. If they were rejected on technical grounds, he would at least have the satisfaction of having placed his apology on the record and of furnishing his biographers with the materials of eulogy. If they were admitted on any grounds at all, he must associate Congress with his defense and might not unreasonably consider himself cleared from censure by the authority most competent to pronounce judgment. If he could induce Congress to pay him interest on his claims, he could salve the wounds of honor with the balm of compensatory damages.

Whether Monroe was well advised in pursuing this course of action is a question that the historian is not called upon to answer. The political philosopher, disregarding the legal aspects of his claims, may ask himself whether the merit or misfortunes of a public officer can form the basis of a claim to the beneficence of his country, and, if so, by what standard the bounty is to be measured. The man of feeling, however, must regret the spectacle of a President of the United States seeking to retort upon the public the injuries that he conceived himself to have received from public characters and from public rumor.

Notes

NOTES TO CHAPTER I

1. *Journal of the House of Representatives*, 18th Congress, 2d Session, p. 110.
2. *Memoirs of John Quincy Adams*, C. F. Adams, ed. (Philadelphia, 1874-1877), VI, 287.
3. I *Register of Debates*, 170-186.
4. *The Writings of James Monroe*, S. M. Hamilton, ed. (New York, 1898-1903), VII, 50.
5. *Writings of James Monroe*, VII, 245.
6. *Memoirs of John Quincy Adams*, VI, 299, 469.
7. *Memoirs of John Quincy Adams*, VI, 444.
8. *Memoirs of John Quincy Adams*, VI, 467.
9. 18th Congress, 2d Session, H. Rep. 79. The committee consisted of Samuel D. Ingham (Pa.), Romulus M. Saunders (N.C.), Joel R. Poinsett (S.C.), Francis Johnson (Ky.), Moses Hayden (N.Y.), Gideon Tomlinson (Conn.), and John Sloane (Ohio). Cocke's papers did not contradict those submitted by Monroe himself.

NOTES TO CHAPTER II

1. The epithet is Martin Van Buren's (*Autobiography*, J. C. Fitzpatrick, ed. [Washington, 1920], p. 769). During the presidential canvass of 1840, Van Buren was charged with having purchased for the presidential mansion some very extravagant French furniture and, among the rest, a parcel of spoons, al-

leged to be of pure gold. The articles complained of were in fact bought for Monroe by Lee. They were vermeil coffee spoons and had cost 115 francs per dozen.

2. 18th Congress, 2d Session, H. Rep. 79, pp. 14-15.
3. William Lee to Burwell Bassett, Feb. 24, 1818; 18th Congress, 2d Session, H. Rep. 79, pp. 244-247.
4. James Monroe to Samuel Lane, April 28, 1817; 18th Congress, 2d Session, H. Rep. 79, p. 240. Mrs. Charles Cotesworth Pinckney had seen part of this furniture in 1796 in Monroe's house in Paris: "Mr. Monroe's furniture is handsome, but as he ordered it with a view to take it to America the chairs are not gilt, and do not suit the rooms." *Letter-book of Mary Stead Pinckney* (New York, 1946), p. 34.
5. 18th Congress, 2d Session, H. Rep. 79, pp. 213-217.
6. This payment exhausted the $20,000 appropriation, for $12,000 had already been advanced to Joseph Russell in France and $2,000 to James Yard in Philadelphia.
7. Russell and La Farge to James Monroe, September 15, 1817, and May 25, 1818; 18th Congress, 2d Session, H. Rep. 79, 159-161, 164-165.
8. Lee to Bassett, Feb. 24, 1818; *ibid.*, p. 245.
9. Monroe to Lane, April 24, 1818; *ibid.*, pp. 240-241.
10. Lane to Monroe; *ibid.*, p. 241.
11. 18th Congress, 2d Session, H. Rep. 79, p. 16.
12. The reader will learn with surprise and, if he be a taxpayer, with envy that the costs of such junkets were not paid out of public funds. Traveling Presidents sponged, like royalty, on the local gentry, accepted free transportation from the mail contractors, but otherwise paid their own way. Monroe stated categorically that the cost of his tours exceeded the sum paid him for his furniture, and that if he had not received the money, he could not have made the inspections.
13. Monroe to Richard Harrison, Feb. 28, 1821; 18th Congress, 2d Session, H. Rep. 79, pp. 241-242.
14. Monroe to Harrison, March 5, 1822; *ibid.*, pp. 247-248.
15. Statement of J. Elgar, Jan. 14, 1824; 18th Congress, 2d Session, H. Rep. 79, pp. 243-244.
16. 18th Congress, 2d Session, H. Rep. 79, pp. 19, 243.
17. Humphrey Peake to Samuel Ingham; *ibid.*, pp. 251-252.

18. *Ibid.*, p. 244. Monroe, who might have remembered the circumstances, preferred to infer them. Speaking of Mr. Carr's evidence, he remarked: "By this it is evident that it [the payment of the note] was not by my desire, nor with my knowledge"; *ibid.*, p. 20.

19. *Ibid.*, pp. 271, 275-277.

20. *Memoirs of John Quincy Adams*, C. F. Adams, ed. (Philadelphia, 1874-1877), VI, 287.

21. 42 *Annals of Congress*, 2609.

22. *Memoirs of John Quincy Adams*, VI, 287.

23. *Memoirs of John Quincy Adams*, VI, 387.

24. John Quincy Adams, who had read all this material before its submission, so greatly misunderstood it that he imagined the President merely to have lent his furniture to the government for a short period in return for a temporary advance of $6,000; *Memoirs of John Quincy Adams*, VI, 289.

25. *Memoirs of John Quincy Adams*, VI, 289. Adams was so impressed by Monroe's experience that when he became President, he made himself personally accountable to the Treasury for the expenditure of the new appropriation for refurnishing the President's house; *ibid.*, VI, 527.

NOTES TO CHAPTER III

1. Daniel C. Gilman, *James Monroe* (Boston, 1890), p. 201; Arthur Styron, *The Last of the Cocked Hats* (Norman, 1945), p. 426; W. P. Cresson, *James Monroe* (Chapel Hill, 1946), pp. 460, 472 ff.

2. By way of comparison it may be noted that until 1799 the salary of the Secretary of State was at the rate of $3,500 per annum. As a Senator, Monroe was receiving $6 a day for every day of his attendance, but might expect a raise to $7 a day beginning March 4, 1795.

3. *Gazette Nationale ou Le Moniteur Universel*, An III, No. 293; *The Autobiography of James Monroe*, S. G. Brown, ed. (Syracuse, 1959), p. 103.

4. Library of Congress, Monroe Papers (1826). In the *Calendar of the Correspondence of James Monroe*, published in 1893 by the Department of State, this memorandum is wrongly ascribed

to Benjamin Vaughan. The endorsement shows that it was sent
to "Mr. Vaughan," but whether Benjamin, John, or the British
minister is not clear. A note identifies it as relating "to my first
mission to France."

5. *Writings of George Washington*, J. C. Fitzpatrick, ed. (Washington, 1931-1944), XXXVI, 216.

6. 19th Congress, 1st Session, H. Doc. 53, p. 7.

7. *Writings of James Monroe*, S. M. Hamilton, ed. (New York,
   1898-1903), III, 90, 123-124, 141-142.

8. See his receipt in the Library of Congress, Monroe Papers.
   B. W. Bond, Jr., the authority on Monroe's first mission to
   France, has mistaken this credit for a payment of money and
   absurdly imagined that it was the first money received by
   Monroe to reimburse him for the expenses of his mission; "The
   Monroe Mission to France," *Johns Hopkins University Studies
   in Historical and Political Science*, XXV, 85.

9. See the copy of the settlement of Monroe's account with the
   bankers of the United States in Holland; Library of Congress,
   Monroe Papers.

10. 18th Congress, 2d Session, H. Rep. 79, p. 5.

11. *Writings of James Monroe*, III, 90.

12. *Writings of James Monroe*, III, 140.

13. *Writings of James Monroe*, III, 141. In the middle of Decem-
    ber 1796, General Pinckney was satisfied that Monroe was no
    longer in office; *Letter-book of Mary Stead Pinckney* (New
    York, 1946), p. 40.

14. *Gazette Nationale ou le Moniteur Universel*, An V, No. 103.
    On leaf 63 of folder 7 of Monroe's manuscript "autobiography
    to 1799," written in 1830, Monroe correctly gives December
    30 as the date of his audience. I am indebted for this informa-
    tion to Mr. Robert W. Hill, Keeper of Manuscripts at the
    New York Public Library.

15. Monroe's secretaries were, seriatim, Fulwar Skipwith, a young
    Frenchman called Gauvain, and John B. Prevost.

16. This allowance was embarrassing to Monroe, for he had paid
    nothing to Prevost to defray his expenses home. But Prevost
    owed him money, and he accepted the credit with appropriate
    explanations to the parties concerned. *Writings of James Mon-
    roe*, III, 148.

17. 19th Congress, 1st Session, H. Doc. 53, p. 9.
18. *Works of Thomas Jefferson*, P. L. Ford, ed. (New York, 1904-1905), IX, 418-421.
19. 18th Congress, 2d Session, H. Rep. 79, pp. 29-30.
20. Napoleon made his decision April 8, the day on which Monroe disembarked at Le Havre. This fact might seem to weaken Monroe's claim to the whole credit of the negotiation—a claim based on the assertion that nothing was done, or could be done, until his arrival. Monroe, however, merely concluded that his coming must have been reported to Napoleon by the telegraph; *The Autobiography of James Monroe*, pp. 155, 166.
21. *Writings of James Monroe*, IV, 106, 161-162.
22. *Letters and other Writings of James Madison* (New York, 1884), II, 192.
23. *Works of Thomas Jefferson*, X, 63.
24. On his first arrival in England, Monroe took a house in Wimpole Street at 500 guineas a year; on his return from Spain, he took a house, first in Great Cumberland Place, later in Portland Place, but always at that price or more; *Writings of James Monroe*, VII, 77.
25. 18th Congress, 2d Session, H. Rep. 79, p. 35
26. *Memoirs of John Quincy Adams*, VII, 539.
27. Hay to Monroe, May 2, 1819; Library of Congress, Monroe Papers. The easy candor of this letter may furnish the reader with a clue to Monroe's own opinion of his brother.
28. *Memoirs of John Quincy Adams*, VI, 445.
29. William Plumer, *Memorandum of Proceedings in the United States Senate*, E. V. Brown, ed. (New York, 1923), pp. 393, 429.
30. *Writings of James Monroe*, V, 53-55.
31. American State Papers, *Foreign Relations*, III, 173-183.
32. *Writings of James Monroe*, V, 120.
33. 19th Congress, 1st Session, H. Doc. 53, p. 13.
34. John Taylor to Monroe, March 12, 1810; Library of Congress, Monroe Papers.
35. 19th Congress, 1st Session, H. Doc. 53, pp. 13-14.
36. That Brent was "apt to be in his cups" was asserted by Sir Augustus John Foster, the British minister to the United States; *Jeffersonian America: Notes on the United States of America Collected in the Years 1805-6-7 and 11-12*, Richard B. Davis,

ed. (San Marino, 1954), pp. 4 n, 72, 100. Foster had instructed an aide to make Brent drunk every day.

37. *Writings of James Monroe*, V, 138.
38. *Works of Thomas Jefferson*, XI, 141.
39. 18th Congress, 2d Session, H. Rep. 79, pp. 26-28, 43-45.
40. *Writings of James Monroe*, V, 194.
41. John Taylor to Monroe, December 6, 1813; Library of Congress, Monroe Papers.
42. 26 *Annals of Congress*, 1383.
43. 18th Congress, 2d Session, H. Rep. 79, pp. 45-47.
44. 18th Congress, 2d Session, H. Rep. 79, pp. 47-49. The assumption that Monroe had written to Pickering on December 6, 1796, was incorrect. He postponed his reply to the Secretary's letter until his return to America in July. *Writings of James Monroe*, III, 67.
45. 19th Congress, 1st Session, H. Doc. 53, pp. 5-6.

NOTES TO CHAPTER IV

1. It would be superfluous to remark that this was *not* a claim for the quarter's salary payable to a minister for returning home, were it not for the fact that some of Monroe's friends so understood it. The allowance for his return had never been in dispute, and Monroe had been granted it as a matter of course.
2. The signers were Joseph Russell, Oliver Champlain, and John Mitchell. Their letters will be found in 18th Congress, 2d Session, H. Rep. 79, pp. 127-128.
3. 18th Congress, 2d Session, H. Rep. 79, pp. 47-50.
4. 19th Congress, 1st Session, H. Rep. 136, pp. 22-23.
5. *The Writings of James Monroe*, S. M. Hamilton, ed. (New York, 1898-1903), III, 63-66.
6. *Writings of James Monroe*, VII, 248.
7. VII *Register of Debates*, 429 (Lewis Williams of North Carolina).
8. *Writings of James Monroe*, III, 24.
9. *Writings of James Monroe*, III, 417.
10. *Writings of George Washington*, J. C. Fitzpatrick, ed. (Washington, 1931-1944), XXXVI, 203 n.

11. *Writings of James Monroe*, III, 96.
12. III *Register of Debates*, 1171.
13. A payment to John H. Purviance for his expenses from Paris to London and back on public business; a payment to Benjamin H. Hichborn for the expenses of an express from Lisbon to Madrid; a payment to Fulwar Skipwith for aid rendered to American seamen.
14. VII *Register of Debates*, 430.
15. Memorandum of April 10, 1823. Quoted by permission of the New York Historical Society, in whose collections the document will be found.
16. In later years Monroe asked for only $3,915 under this head of account—interest on $9,000 at 6 per cent for seven years and three months—January 1803 to April 1810. It seems probable that in 1825 he counted eight years and three months by mistake.
17. 18th Congress, 2d Session, H. Rep. 79, pp. 35-36.
18. 18th Congress, 2d Session, H. Rep. 79, p. 6 n. The allowance to King was actually at the rate of $1,555 a year, not $1,740, as calculated by Monroe.
19. I *Register of Debates*, 95.
20. VII *Register of Debates*, 432.
21. 18th Congress, 2d Session, H. Rep. 79, p. 46.
22. Quoted by permission of the New York Historical Society, in whose collections the document is preserved.
23. Adams thought the decision to have been made, not on the merits of the claim, but on personal and political grounds. Clay was a powerful man and an insidious enemy of the Administration. *Memoirs of John Quincy Adams*, C. F. Adams, ed. (Philadelphia, 1874-1877), V, 311, 329. When a son of James A. Bayard, as executor of his father's will, came to Adams in 1824 with a similar claim, the latter referred him to the President, "who had made the allowance to Mr. Clay, after taking the opinion of the Attorney General, and against mine"; *ibid.*, VI, 261. William Wirt, who knew nothing about the subject of such claims, pleaded unsuccessfully with Monroe to refer it to the Cabinet; Library of Congress, Monroe Papers.
24. In his memoir to the Ingham committee, Monroe stated only his general idea as to when interest should commence. In his

public memoir, printed in December 1826, he gave precision to that idea; *Writings of James Monroe*, VII, 267-268.

25. VII *Register of Debates*, 433.

26. VII *Register of Debates*, 432. Lewis Williams was pointing these remarks at Monroe, but they constituted nevertheless an accurate statement of the usage which a Comptroller of the Treasury in 1813 had found to be "coeval with the first formation of the Government." 26 *Annals of Congress*, 793. Comptroller Richard Rush noticed that the rule regarding interest was reciprocal; if the government refused interest to its creditors, it never charged any to its debtors.

27. *Writings of James Monroe*, VII, 19.

28. *Memoirs of John Quincy Adams*, VI, 276, 282.

NOTES TO CHAPTER V

1. *The Writings of James Monroe*, S. M. Hamilton, ed. (New York, 1898-1903), VII, 57.

2. Marshall to Monroe, July 13, 1825; Library of Congress, Monroe Papers.

3. II *Register of Debates*, 846-852. This was Willie P. Mangum of North Carolina, a man remembered in 1855 "only for his consolidation Whiggery and his excessive devotion to his potations"; *South Carolina Legislative Times* (Columbia, 1855), p. 98.

4. 19th Congress, 1st Session, H. Rep. 136. The members were Samuel D. Ingham (Pa.), Romulus M. Saunders (N.C.), Francis Johnson (Ky.), Moses Hayden (N.Y.), Gideon Tomlinson (Conn.), John Sloane (Ohio), and George McDuffie (S.C.).

NOTES TO CHAPTER VI

1. Monroe's agent in Washington was his son-in-law, Samuel L. Gouverneur.

2. Monroe to Tench Ringgold, May 8, 1826; *Writings of James Monroe*, S. M. Hamilton, ed. (New York, 1898-1903), VII, 83-84.

3. The remarks were written while the claims were under consideration; where they appear to be inconsistent with the memoir, as in the claiming and disclaiming of an indemnity or

punitive damages, the explanation may be sought in Monroe's changed circumstances.

4. John McLean to Monroe, Nov. 11, 1826; Library of Congress, Monroe Papers.
5. *Memoirs of John Quincy Adams*, C. F. Adams, ed. (Philadelphia, 1874-1877), VII, 218-219.
6. John McLean to Monroe, Feb. 1, 1827; Library of Congress, Monroe Papers. At a Jackson dinner in New York, held early in 1827, Monroe's name was omitted from the toasts. S. L. Southard to Monroe, Feb. 4, 1827; Library of Congress, Monroe Papers.
7. According to Jackson, Monroe helped to create the impression that, in order to save New Orleans, he had had to order Jackson to retrace his steps after he had started home; *Correspondence of Andrew Jackson*, J. S. Barrett and J. F. Jameson, eds. (Washington, 1926-1935), IV, 339.
8. III *Register of Debates*, 1165-1176.
9. John McLean to Monroe, March 21 and 24, 1828; Library of Congress, Monroe Papers.
10. McLean to Monroe, Aug. 2, 1828; Library of Congress, Monroe Papers.
11. Monroe to McLean, Aug. 7, 1828; Library of Congress, Monroe Papers.
12. *Writings of James Monroe*, VII, 189-192.
13. 20th Congress, 2d Session, H. Doc. 94.
14. A quarter of 1 per cent was the usual commission.
15. William C. Rives (Va.), chairman, Samuel D. Ingham (Pa.), Rudolph Bunner (N.J.), Tristam Burges (R.I.), Samuel P. Carson (N.C.), John Taliaferro (Va.), and John Davis (Mass.).
16. 20th Congress, 2d Session, H. Rep. 76.
17. The details can be reconstructed from Account A attached to Fifth Auditor's Report (No. 2,597), April 12, 1831; National Archives, General Records Division.
18. *Revue Universelle des Arts*, XII, p. 353. A description of the house is in the *Letter-book of Mary Stead Pinckney* (New York, 1946).
19. Camille Piton, *Paris sous Louis XV* (Paris, 1914), V, 132-135; G. Capon and R. Yves-Plessis, *Fille d'Opéra, Vendeuse d'-Amour* (Paris, 1906), pp. 111-114.
20. *Bulletin de la Société de l'Histoire de Paris* (1930-1931), p. 297.

21. Gerry to Monroe, April 4, 1797; Library of Congress, Monroe Papers.
22. *Writings of James Monroe*, III, 145.
23. *Letters and other Writings of James Madison* (New York, 1884), II, 92.
24. *Writings of James Monroe*, III, 138, 145. In 1801 he secured affidavits of his intention from William Lee, General William Hull, and Benjamin Hichborn; in 1825 he supplemented these by an affidavit from Fulwar Skipwith; *ibid.*, VII, 287-290.
25. According to Moufle d'Angerville (*Vie Privée de Louis XV*, I, 278), the Folie La Bouexière was a "palais énorme. . . . L'édifice est sans goût, mal distribué; les dedans sont d'une richesse immense. Il y a pour 25,000 livres de bras de cheminée et pour 60,000 livres de glaces. Il n'y a que six pièces. Ce Louvre se réduit à un petit appartement de garçon."
26. Harper to Giles, May 30 and June 14, 1797; Library of Congress, Monroe Papers.
27. 20th Congress, 2d Session, H. Rep. 96.
28. Deposition of Tench Ringgold, Feb. 14, 1826; *Writings of James Monroe*, VII, 306-309. The notion advanced by John Quincy Adams in his *Eulogy on the Life and Character of James Monroe*, that Monroe obtained funds for the defense of New Orleans "by pledging his private individual credit, as subsidiary to that of the nation," cannot be entertained. In eulogies, as in lapidary inscriptions, a man is not upon oath. "The pretension," said General Armstrong, "improbable in itself, is rendered utterly incredible, by what is known of the practice and principles of money lenders; by what is believed to have been the condition of Mr. Monroe's pecuniary means and credit, at that period," etc. *Notice of Mr. Adams' Eulogium*, p. 35. See also X *Register of Debates*, 1951, 1975-1976.
29. 28 *Annals of Congress*, 656.
30. Mercer was, of course, the chairman. The other members were George McDuffie (S.C.), Samuel P. Carson (N.C.), Richard Coulter (Pa.), John Davis (Mass.), John Taliaferro (Va.), and George E. Mitchell (Md.).
31. 21st Congress, 1st Session, H. Rep. 276.
32. VII *Register of Debates*, 446.
33. VI *Register of Debates*, 1140.

34. Hugh Nelson to Monroe, June 28, 1830; Library of Congress, Monroe Papers.
35. The editor of Jackson's *Correspondence* (IV, 205, n. 5) is inclined to place this dinner in November 1830. Lewis' own statement that it was given in November 1829 is corroborated by John Quincy Adams (*Memoirs*, VIII, 317, 320), who in February 1831 mentioned it as having occurred "last winter." According to A. J. Donelson, Jackson's private secretary, Ringgold, in revealing this secret of the Cabinet, was attempting to predispose Jackson in favor of Monroe's claim by gaining access to his prejudice against Calhoun; *Correspondence of Andrew Jackson*, IV, 205.
36. *Memoirs of John Quincy Adams*, VIII, 250.
37. 21st Congress, 2d Session, H. Doc. 6.
38. These documents are preserved in the manuscript papers of the House of Representatives, access to which was allowed me by courtesy of the Honorable Ralph R. Roberts, Clerk of the House.
39. Sergeant to Gouverneur, Dec. 27, 1830; Library of Congress, Monroe Papers.
40. *Memoirs of John Quincy Adams*, VIII, 258-259. According to Nicholas Biddle, Burrows "had been very liberal to Mr. Monroe in his pecuniary misfortunes." X *Register of Debates*, 134. He appears to have loaned him a thousand dollars; *Memoirs of John Quincy Adams*, VIII, 258.
41. Robert Y. Hayne (S.C.), chairman, Nathan Sanford (N.Y.), Theodore Frelinghuysen (N.J.), Samuel Bell (N.H.), and James Iredell (N.C.). The two Senators last named voted against the bill. It was perhaps fortunate for Monroe that Senator James Noble of Indiana, who had expressed a decided opinion against its ultimate passage, had on February 26 gone to his last reward.
42. VII *Register of Debates*, 216.
43. *Writings of James Monroe*, VII, 233.
44. Monroe's correspondence and accounts relative to this business are preserved in the 5th Auditor's account, No. 2597, dated April 12, 1831; National Archives, General Records Division, Record Group 217. I am indebted to Mr. Lyle J. Holverstott, Archivist in Charge, Fiscal Branch, for aid in finding them.

45. Fifth's Auditor's Report, No. 2597, dated April 7, 1831. Mr. Laurence Gouverneur Hoes, a direct descendant of Monroe's, has kindly permitted me to examine his copy of this report.
46. Fifth's Auditor's Report, No. 2597, dated April 12, 1831.
47. *Writings of James Monroe*, VII, 232 n.
48. *Memoirs of John Quincy Adams*, VIII, 360.
49. Library of Congress, Monroe Papers.
50. Library of Congress, Monroe Papers.

NOTES TO CHAPTER VII

1. Jefferson to William Temple Franklin, May 7, 1786; *The Papers of Thomas Jefferson*, Julian P. Boyd, ed. (Princeton, 1950-), IX, 466. Compare Jefferson's character of William Stephens Smith: "For his *honesty* he is like our friend *Monroe*. Turn his *soul* wrong side outwards and there is not a speck on it." Jefferson to James Madison, Jan. 30, 1787; *ibid.*, XI, 97.
2. *Memoirs of John Quincy Adams*, C. F. Adams, ed. (Philadelphia, 1874-1877), VIII, 360.
3. 18th Congress, 2d Session, H. Rep. 79, p. 127 n.
4. IV *Register of Debates*, 1205.
5. IV *Register of Debates*, 1305.
6. IV *Register of Debates*, 1288.
7. 20th Congress, 2d Session, H. Doc. 94, p. 2.
8. 21st Congress, 2d Session, H. Doc. 6, p. 1.
9. By Clement Dorsey, Representative from Maryland, a friend of Monroe's; IV *Register of Debates*, 1258.
10. VII *Register of Debates*, 606. A similar jest, applied to Governor Yates of New York, is related in Van Buren's *Autobiography*, J. C. Fitzpatrick, ed. (Washington, 1920), p. 148.
11. II *Register of Debates*, 405.
12. II *Register of Debates*, 2629; VII *Register of Debates*, 329.
13. Political Disquisitions, New Series, Nos. III-V; VII *Register of Debates*, 439. Giles suggested that Monroe's presidential construction of the appropriating power of Congress was a novelty designed to fit precisely the case of his own extraordinary claims.
14. *Scientific and Literary Repository*, Nos. V and VI.